For Claudio, Fabrizio and Maia

Acknowledgments

This book would not have been possible without the unconditional support of dozens of Turkish chefs and food lovers, who selflessly accompanied me throughout the project process, providing their knowledge and cooking their most valuable recipes with me.

Also fundamental was the work of Beatriz Garlaschi, who, through the lens of her camera, helped me capture the essence of this culinary journey in an exceptional way.

To my family, who gave me all the necessary support and patience, in addition to venturing with me on different trips to the interior of the country in order to gather the necessary information for the development of this book.

But my main gratitude is undoubtedly to Filiz Hösükoglu, expert and reference in the country in Turkish gastronomy and who inspired me to embark on this wonderful project and, furthermore, inspired me with her characteristic enthusiasm about Turkish gastronomy. With her, I discovered the best-kept secrets of this impressive culture. I would like to dedicate this book to her, with all my gratitude.

Finally, I cannot thank enough the people of Turkey who opened their kitchens to delight me every day with their colorful dishes, their wonderful spices and their unparalleled kindness.

Special acknowledgements

Turkish Culinary Academy, Semi Çiloğullari, Borges Café, Erzurum Çağ Kebab, Torum Carpets, Sefa Torum, Celik Çay Ocağı.

ISBN: 978-1-66785-273-7

Design by: Geoffrey Arias
Edited by: Jacqueline Pierantoni
Proof-reading: Miriam Polito de Fabiancic
Photographers: Beatriz Garlashi and Alicia Santana

ALATURKA

A journey through Turkish Gastronomy, its history and
its most iconic recipes, told by local chefs

Alicia Santana

ALATURKA

A journey through Turkish Gastronomy, its history and
its most iconic recipes, told by local chefs

CONTENTS

CONTENTS

Photo by Fatih Yürür

Kokoreç vendor at Ulus
—Antındağ – Ankara

INTRODUCTION

Turkish food is not just food; it is art. An art form refined by hundreds of years of practice and awareness of its origins.

The precision with which Turkish people prepare the meat for the kebabs; the technique they use when kneading the dough for the baklava and katmer; the particular way they dry the vegetables for conservation during winter months; the respect they have for their ingredients and utensils, as well as how they present their dishes and serve food on the table, do not go unnoticed by food lovers.

It is an art that Turks learn at home, from a young age, and as a family, because the key attribute of Turkish cuisine is that it is meant to be shared with loved ones.

The preparation of its impressive 'kahvaltı' (Turkish breakfast), the wide variety of its 'mezes' (appetizers) and the thousands of delicious and unique recipes are just some examples of this art. Also, the love with which they prepare the dumplings for their famous 'yuvarlama' (page 115), a dish as complex as it is delicious, and served in Gaziantep in southeast Anatolia, is capable of promoting the unity of the family in the kitchen with its celebration of life through food.

In every Turkish kitchen, people use instruments and techniques in the same way their ancestors did. Recipes are respected and protected, and the use of Turkish ingredients is promoted.

The vast majority of people I have been lucky enough to cook with have all answered in the same way, when asked where they learned to prepare their delicious dishes: 'I learned it from my mother.' It is as if it were the actual duty of families to not let the gastronomic heritage they have inherited and honed over the years, be lost. If that is the case, they have most definitely succeeded.

In Turkey even the least experienced of cooks can still tell you how to prepare a 'kısır' (page 151) or which ingredients cannot be left out of, or are vital to, the 'dolmas' (page 111). They may not have had much practice, but the truth is that they have plenty of innate knowledge.

My intention in writing this book has been to share a little of that wich Turkish cuisine has to offer. Dismissed by many to be little more than kebabs and baklava, it is, in fact, a hugely varied and vastly influential cuisine.

Many ancient civilizations passed through what is now Turkey, shaping and dramatically enhancing its cuisine. A cuisine which, in turn, has influenced how people cook in far-flung and unimaginable corners of the globe. For example, it is Turkey we must thank for fermenting milk and creating yoghurt, a modern-day breakfast staple. This is just one of the hundreds of ingredients and culinary techniques that were born in the lands of Anatolia, and that today form part of world cuisine.

To do full justice to Turkish gastronomy, dozens of huge volumes would be needed. With this book, I only intend to contribute with my grain of sand and share what Turkey gave me during the five wonderful years I lived there, during which Turks opened the doors of their kitchens to share with me some of their most valuable secrets.

WHY WRITE THIS BOOK?

When I learned that we would have to pack up and move to Turkey with my family because of my husband's work, I knew nothing more about the country than that which I had read in my school history books.

❧

When I learned that we would have to pack up and move to Turkey with my family because of my husband's work, I knew nothing more about the country than that which I had read in my school history books.

I am from the Dominican Republic, a country in the Caribbean, a region generally influenced by western culture (Europe and the United States). My only point of reference to the Middle East at that time was the contact our island has with Lebanon, due to the large Lebanese community that migrated to the region in the late 19th and early 20th centuries. Needless to say, Turkey was not exactly on my radar. In the Dominican Republic, the descendants of these immigrant groups, generally from Mount Lebanon, are still often called 'the Turks' because the passports or safe-conducts they used to travel with were Turkish, as in those days the Ottoman Empire (Turks) occupied the whole region. (Alvarez, 2018)

Before traveling, I asked many people about this, for me, undiscovered country, and, to my surprise, their answers were slightly opaque and not wholly positive. Turning instead to books and the internet, my family and I began to get a better idea of where destiny was taking us.

We started with travel books. We bought a couple and started to read them. It is not my place to question the lack of accuracy and knowledge of those who claimed to know Turkey, but what I can tell you, is that having read and taken these books at face value, the idea of moving our family's life to such a country terrified me. Fortunately, as things turned out, reality proved quite different!

Being a food lover, my interest soon turned to gastronomy. Until then, the only Turkish dishes I had ever tried were the Turkish 'döner' kebabs prepared by a Pakistani family in Italy, or the 'westernized' kebabs sold on the streets of New York, or the baklava made for us once in Nicaragua by a Greek friend.

What I saw on the internet about Turkish cuisine, on the other hand, immediately caught my attention. I could not, for obvious reasons, associate the photos with an aroma, a flavor, or a texture, but I began to imagine the Turkey I wanted to discover.

My first contact with the country

I remember the first time I saw her, from above. We were arriving on a direct flight from Munich. We landed in Ankara in mid-August 2016. A semi-desertic landscape. Warm, immense, bathed by a special light. It was a temperature that, to us, arriving after four wonderful years in sultry Cuba, seemed ideal. A dry, yet fresh air, filled with a combination of new aromas that we could not yet describe.

And there they were; the Turks. From the moment we stepped out onto the ground, people embraced us with their smiles and their kindness. They made us feel like we had just arrived home, to a home that we did not even know we had. Immediately, all stress of the last two months began to fade.

Once in Turkey, we realized that the Turkish-Pakistani-Italian kebab and the kebab in New York, despite its fascinating taste, did not even come close to the delicacy prepared by Turks in Turkey. We soon learned that baklava was a dessert that made sense only when enjoyed in a town called Gaziantep, in Southeast Turkey. And so began our incredible journey of discovery.

A Brief History of Turkish Gastronomy

A gastronomy with plenty of history

One of the richest worldwide, Turkish food culture owes its wealth to its history, geographical location, and varied climate. Over time, different cultures have settled in or passed through these beautiful lands, all of them leaving behind part of their cultural heritage. Their traditions have contributed to the Turkish gastronomic wealth that we enjoy today.

The arrival of nomadic immigrants from Central Asia brought with it a culture of hunting and livestock. Part of their legacy is the way sausages are prepared today and how Turks conserve meat in winter, firstly by cooking it in its fat and then by storing it in cubes, just as Pastirma is prepared nowadays. It was in this period that the heirs of the Anatolian lands inherited milk and yogurt and started to use wheat, molasses, and vinegar. From that time onwards it became customary to eat horse, camel, goat and sheep (mutton) together with their giblets, cooked in a Tandoor. Although the food at that time was simple, the period still managed to bequeath a culture of kebab-making to the Turkish people.

During the Seljuk immigration of the 12th century, Islam was adopted as a religion along with part of the Arab culinary culture. The consumption of pork, hoofed animals, reptiles and shellfish such as crab, lobster and mollusks was forbidden and wiped out. The Seljuks introduced many new species as well as the use of spices. Meat consumed during this period was mostly mutton, goat, fish and poultry. The Seljuks also introduced to the region the idea of eating eggs.

New meat preparation techniques were brought in, namely stew, pilaf and bulgur.

During the rule of the Otoman Empire, following the conquest of Constantinople (today Istanbul) in 1453, the palace and the public kitchen were separated. Fatih Sultan Mehmed imported cooks and ingredients from other parts of the empire, giving way to more complex gastronomy. Ingredients such as lentils, leeks, cabbage, spinach, tomato, and nuts were imported. It was customary to have only two meals; breakfast early in the morning and dinner, eaten just before sunset. People generally ate with their hands or perhaps with a single spoon at the beginning of this period. Later, tables, chairs, forks and knives were added.

After Turkey was proclaimed a republic in 1923, there was a rapprochement with western culture and ingredients such as asparagus, tomato paste, corn, margarine, cocoa, olive oil, black tea, and carbonated drinks were introduced. Veal and beef were added to the menu. New sauces and accompaniments made their debut. It was then that Turkish gastronomy began to be studied from two different angles: 'the kitchen of the people' and 'the classic kitchen', the latter referring to the cuisine that had emerged previously in the Ottoman palace.

Although some of these gastronomic customs have disappeared over time, many still remain.

Above: Turkish Sucuk at Ulus market – Ankara
Below: Pastirma

Wealth in geographical diversity

✥

Turkish territory, which covers some 785,350 km2, has a vast biodiversity with climates that vary greatly from one region to another. Turkey's biological diversity can be compared to that of a small continent thanks to its location. Within its boundaries lie all manner of forests, mountains, savannas, wetlands, coastal and marine ecosystems.

From the rainy and fertile climate of the Black Sea region, where nuts and black tea are grown as well as corn, kiwi, rice, beans, and potatoes, one moves to the Marmara region, the bridge between Europe and Asia, whose regular rains facilitate the growth of several fruits and where about 73% of the sunflowers and 30% of the country's corn are produced. Local products include wheat, rice, olives, and vineyards.

In the Aegean region, with its coastline characterized by crystalline beaches and blessed with a mild climate, olive groves abound. This region is home to almost half the olive trees in Turkey and, needless to say, produces excellent olive oil.

As for the Mediterranean region, the flat terrain and warm climate of the Mediterranean Sea give rise to a very fertile land. This characteristic makes it suitable for the cultivation of citrus, grapes, cereals, and rice. In this region, 80% of Turkish oranges and clementines are grown. In Central Anatolia, however, the terrain is generally arid due to low rainfall. Despite this, the climate of Anatolia still allows for the cultivation of barley, as well as one-third of the country's wheat production.

A series of hot springs and numerous rivers are to be found in Turkey. Although a few do flow through to neighboring countries, most of them are fully contained within Turkey, their deltas nourishing and creating a ripe and fertile land.

TURKEY AND ITS SPICES

A Short History of Spices

Records show that since early times herbs, leaves, roots, and seeds have been used medicinally and as condiments. Ancient civilizations wrapped the meat they hunted in leaves and herbs to protect it from being spoiled. It was thus that they made a huge discovery. The meat remained preserved for longer periods and its flavor was improved, while bad odors were disguised. The essence of leaves, seeds, flowers and other parts of the plants transferring to the food. That is how humanity discovered spices.

In ancient China, Pen Ts'ao Chung's treatise 'The Classic Herbal' of 2700 BC mentions the use of spices such as cassia and cinnamon in medicinal practices. In India, spices such as cinnamon, black pepper, turmeric, cardamom, mustard, sesame, ginger and cloves have been used for thousands of years in medicinal practices, spiritual rites, cooking, and as digestion aids.

Spices were traded during biblical times and used for religious offerings, burial rituals, and improving health. In various chapters of the Bible, spices such as cinnamon, saffron, coriander seeds, mint, dill, and cumin are mentioned, both in the Old and New Testaments.

Although mention is made of cardamom and cinnamon being used to improve the taste of food in Ancient Egypt, spices were mainly used for medicinal and cosmetic purposes. The Eber Papyrus (1500 BC) recorded medical treatments using cloves, mint, fennel, caraway, poppy seeds, coriander, garlic, onion, and peppermint. Workers used onion and garlic during the construction of the Great Pyramid of Cheops in Giza to promote stamina and improve health. Even some traces of garlic were found in Tutankhamun's tomb.

Ancient cuneiforms from Mesopotamia recorded the cultivation of spices and aromatic herbs on the banks of the Tigris and Euphrates rivers. The Sumerians (3rd Millennium BC), Assyrians (668–633 BC) and Babylonians (721–710 BC) recorded the use of thyme, sesame, cardamom, turmeric, saffron, poppy seeds, coriander, garlic, anise, dill, and myrrh in medicinal practices. The Persians (559–529 BC), for their part, used onion, garlic, and shallot to enhance the flavor of their meals.

The ancient Greeks imported pepper, cassia, cinnamon, ginger, caraway, fennel, coriander, mint, garlic, parsley, and marjoram. They used a vast number of spices in their medicine, bread, wine, and cooking. Hippocrates, the father of modern medicine, (460–377 BC) wrote down at least four-hundred herbal remedies.

The ancient Romans used spices in abundance. They used them in their wines, fragrances, and in oils for their famous baths. Although they had used caraway, onion, rosemary, and thyme since ancient times, they now imported spices, like pepper, from the East.

For the Arabs and Muslims, spices represented a valuable commodity. They applied advanced distillation techniques to extract essential oils from herbs and spices with which they then created syrups and extracts. The Spice Route was established with Arabia during the Roman Empire. In this period the Arabs managed to maintain their monopoly over spices by making up stories about extremely poisonous flying snakes that they claimed protected the spice crops. This succeeded in discouraging the Europeans from looking too hard for the source of the supply and kept its whereabouts secret. In this way, they were able to maintain the high prices of the spices.

The Spice Trade Routes

Together the Silk Route and the Spice Route represent two of the most important trade routes in the history of mankind. Although their goods and points of origin were different, the destination and main part of the routes were the same (especially in the region that corresponds to Anatolia).

Thanks to them, not only was there a steady flow of trade between Asia and Europe, but also a constant exchange of meaningful social, political and cultural interaction between the two continents. In addition to the exchange of goods, the countries along the route shared technological developments. Needless to say, the gastronomy of the countries along these routes also underwent substantial changes.

In this period, spices such as cardamom, black pepper, cinnamon, and turmeric were transported from Asia to Europe. These spices, considered as luxury goods thanks to their high cost, reached Europe by two different routes.

Departing from the Moluccan or 'Spice' Islands in Indonesia, the spices were then transported, mainly by sea, to the coasts of Southern India and Sri Lanka, where they were traded with Arab merchants. From there, the spices were transported across the Persian Gulf to Iraq. Later, they continued their journey overland in caravans.

In a second route, the spices were transported to Egypt via the Red Sea and Suez Canal, to the city of Alexandria, on the Mediterranean. They were then taken by sea to ports in Palestine and Syria and then onwards, by caravan, to the Black Sea and on to Europe.

The territory of Anatolia, which we now know as modern Turkey, was strategically located along this route. Bridging Asia with Europe, it could take full advantage of any trade and commerce. The prominence given today to the use of spices in Turkey derives undoubtedly from this event. Furthermore, the areas along the route are the very ones who still use spices pre-eminently in their gastronomy.

Turkish Gastronomy Today

The greatness of Turkish cuisine did not come about by coincidence, but rather because of the country's strategic geographical location, enviable climatic conditions, and millennial history.

As we saw in the previous chapter, exotic ingredients were transported from Indonesia, India, and China and were later traded by Arab merchants to be sold to the Venetians. A large part of these ingredients passed through Anatolia. A wider cultural exchange also took place, in which art and gastronomy played a fundamental role.

The occupation of Anatolia by civilizations such as the Hittites, Seljuks, Byzantines, and Ottomans also influenced the vast gastronomy of Turkey today.

The culture of preserving food came about as a response to both climatic conditions and from the need to keep vegetables and meat safe and available to eat during the long caravan trips that occurred at that time. In the same way, the tradition of cooking meat over fire and the specific way of preparing kebabs may be another legacy of these ancient civilizations, which, lacking, or ignoring, perhaps, more complex techniques, simply took advantage of what they had at hand.

Vegetables dried in the sun in summer, to be stuffed and consumed in winter (dolmas – page 111), fermented soups reduced to powder (Tarhana – page 76), the way to preserve meat in Pastirma and suçuks, as well as the appearance of yogurt are just a few examples of their food culture. Similarly, there are vegetables preserved in oil or in a mixture of vinegar and salt (pickles) common in Turkey that are served today with meat dishes.

While the main influences came from countries in the Middle East and Central Asia, others came instead from North Africa and Europe. A vast number of spices and techniques were imported during the Silk Trade Route years and added to food preservation and meat preparation, as in the case of kebabs and stews. New ingredients such as tomatoes, chili, corn, and beans also arrived from Europe. These ingredients, recently discovered in the New World, arrived in Turkey thanks to the importance given during the Ottoman empire to the creation of a more modern and enhanced cuisine.

Therefore, Persian, Asian, and European influences can all be recognized in the Turkish cuisine we know today. All mixed together in a combination of flavors and all adding to the complexity of this sensational gastronomy.

Colors and Aromas in Turkish Gastronomy today

In Turkish gastronomy, different spices frame the history of each region. That is why the areas along the Spice Route are precisely those where the use of spices is more dominant. Such is the case of Antakya, Adana, Gaziantep, Mardin, Sanliurfa, Diyarbakir, and Bursa; all renowned for using several spices in their dishes.

All Turkish cities use spices in their cooking to some extent, resulting in the mouth-watering aromas emanating from Turkish kitchens.

Turkish spread. By Sonya-Kamoz

HOW THE TURKISH USE SPICES

Dry spices are ubiquitous in Turkish cuisine, in seed, flake, root or powdered form. Spices such as şumak, cumin, mint, and sweet and spicy red chili are fundamental to its main recipes. In many cases, more than one spice is used in a single dish, resulting in complex and strongly accentuated flavors.

ŞUMAK
(Rhus)

Şumak is the fruit of a shrub that bears its name.
In Turkey it is generally harvested in August and September,
and then dried before being consumed as a spice.

Countries such as Iran, Afghanistan, as well as Southeast Europe, North Africa, and the Mediterranean currently produce this spice. In Turkey, şumak grows almost everywhere, except for Eastern Anatolia.

Şumak has an intense dark red color and usually has a bitter taste when in its natural state. After being dried and mixed with salt, the taste turns saltier, with only a slight hint of bitterness.

It can be consumed as seeds, as flakes, or as a powder. It is also prepared in liquid form, which gives it a more concentrated taste. Its smell is lemony, with a touch of licorice.

In Turkey, şumak is one of the most used and appreciated spices due to its sour taste which helps to enhance salads and various traditional dishes. In cities like Adana, in the Mediterranean region, şumak is added to the famous red onion salad which accompanies their signature dish, the Adana Kebab (page 147).

It can be used as a seasoning for salads and to add a slight acidity to some recipes. It can also be consumed as tea and juice.

YENIBAHAR
(All spice)

Yenibahar (Allspice) is a spice native to Jamaica and is used in Turkish cuisine in the preparation of some meat dishes, especially köfte (meatballs).

It is known as allspice in English because the smell and taste of this spice recall others such as cinnamon, cloves, and nutmeg. It also has a slight minty scent and taste.

The fruits of this spice are harvested before they ripen and are left to dry in the sun. Once dry, the fruit turns a light brown color, a sign that it is ready for eating.

In the southeastern part of Turkey, Yenibahar is used in the preparation of the famous dolma (stuffed vegetables). It is also used in a variety of desserts, including Aşure, also known as the 'peace' dessert. Legend has it that when Noah's Ark came to rest on Mount Ararat in Eastern Turkey, the event was celebrated with a dish concocted from whatever ingredients were to hand, thus creating this pleasing dessert that is made on the tenth day of Muharram (first month at the Islamic calendar) and is shared with relatives and neighbors.

TOZ PUL BIBER

(Red pepper powder)

Toz pul biber is undoubtedly the most used spice in Turkish cuisine.

🐦

It can be sweet (tatlı pul biber), prepared with capia red peppers, or hot (acı toz pul biber) prepared with a mixture of hot chili peppers.

The preparation process is the same. After washing the chilies well, they are deveined, and the seeds removed. After that, the chilies are put out to dry in the sun for a minimum of ten days and later, they are ground and passed through a sieve. A little olive oil and salt are usually added to this chili powder.

The pul biber is used in all types of cooking. It is added to meat dishes, soups and stir-fries. It is used for its aroma but also to add a hint of color. It is one of the spices that can always be found in homes and restaurants throughout Turkey, perfect for adding that final touch of bittersweet to meals.

KIRMIZI PUL BIBER

(Flaked Red pepper)

🐦

Like toz pul biber, kirmizi pul biber is commonly used in Turkish cuisine. It is generally hot and is added to some kebabs to increase their spiciness. It is usually made with hot chili peppers and by the same process as the one used to prepare powdered red pepper, except for the fact that they aren't ground so finely.

ISOT
(Isot pepper)

Isot is a spice produced from a red chili grown in Sanliurfa, in Southeastern Turkey.

The fresh peppers are harvested in summer and, after having had their seeds and veins removed, they are dried in the sun. Once dry, they are placed in a plastic bag and laid out in the sun. They are then dampened with hot water every day. The humidity produced by the effect of the sun on the closed bag gives the chili its dark color. Subsequently, the chilies are ground with a pestle and mixed with olive oil and salt, then passed through a sieve to remove any residue. In summer, the roofs of Sanliurfa are covered with chili peppers drying in the sun.

Isot enhances the taste of meat recipes, such as Lahmacun, a kind of flatbread covered with meat which is served throughout the country. To produce a single kilogram of Isot, you need at least ten kilograms of fresh chili, so this spice is usually slightly more expensive than ordinary chili powder.

Its smell, like its flavor, is intense and a little smoky. It has a slightly bitter taste. Although it may not necessarily be considered one of the hottest spices on the planet, you can still feel the spiciness rising from the tip of your tongue when you eat it, and it certainly gives dishes a bit of extra kick.

NANE
(Mint)

Together with pul biber and şumak, nane is the third spice you will find most often on Turkish dining tables.

It is mostly used dry, then it is generally fried in butter and added as the last touch to yogurt-based dishes and some soups. It is also used in the preparation of dolmas, some mezes and to enhance some salads.

Fresh from the garden, its leaves are also used in countless salads for their fresh flavor and comforting aroma. It is often added to enhance the taste of lemonade.

KIMYON
(Cumin)

This super aromatic spice, known worldwide and hard to miss in a dish, is widely used in Turkish cuisine.

Although cumin is primarily used in its powdered form, it can also be used in seeds.

With a slightly bitter taste, its aroma is used to enhance various meat and rice dishes. It is also used when making dolmas. Cumin has been produced and used in Turkey since the Hittite period.

KÖFTE BAHARI
(Meatball spices)

Is a mix of spices that combines coriander seeds, black pepper, hot red pepper, sweet red pepper, turmeric, cumin, sumac and ginger.

Köfte baharı is used to flavor dishes such as the famous Turkish köfte, as well as some rice dishes and dishes containing ground meat. It is a powdered spice that you can find in any supermarket or spice market in Turkey.

Other spices commonly used in Turkish cuisine are coriander seeds (kişniş), mustard (hardal) seeds, black pepper (karabiber), thyme (kekik), rosemary (biberiye), and bay leaves (defne yaprakları). Cinnamon (tarçın), ginger (zencefil), and cloves (karanfiller) are also used widely across the country. Many of these spices add aroma and color and significantly enhance the rich flavor that characterizes Turkish gastronomy.

OTHER TYPICAL INGREDIENTS USED IN TURKISH CUISINE

BIBER SALÇASI
(Sweet pepper paste)

Red pepper paste is used almost daily.
It is often mixed in equal measure with tomato paste.

Fresh pepper of the Capia type is used to make it and from which all veins, seeds, and stems must be removed. This pepper is cooked for a half-hour in a pot with a bit of water and rock salt; then it's blended and strained well to remove any residues from the skin. Afterwards, the paste is placed on a tray and sun-dried for at least two days so that the excess water evaporates. Finally, salt and olive oil are added for conservation.

In a country where winters are usually long and harsh, it is vital that summer vegetables are sun-dried so that they can be conserved and kept ready to eat in the cold season.

This paste is used, for example, in the Turkish version of muhammara (page 62). This meze is widely consumed in Turkey, and instead of being prepared with fresh and roasted peppers as is customary in other countries with more temperate climates, the Turks use the preserved ones. The same happens with eggplants, ubiquitous in Turkish Cuisine. During the summer, they are roasted, peeled, and preserved in jars. This Turkish wonder, which makes life easier for thousands of families, can be found in supermarkets all over the country, and its taste and texture have nothing to envy those prepared fresh at home.

ÜZÜM PEKMEZI

(grape molasses)

Thanks to its climate and the richness and variety of its soil, Turkey has produced high-quality grapes for thousands of years.

In documents found in the excavations of Hittite ruins, mention is made of vineyards and the use of their fruits in different recipes, particularly juices. 20% of the annual production of grapes in the country is destined to become molasses.

Üzüm pekmezi was used to sweeten dishes long before sugar took over as the global sweetener of choice. Pekmez (molasses) is a dense, dark liquid produced from the caramelization of grapes. This ingredient is crucial to Turkish food culture. It is eaten mainly at breakfast, sometimes mixed with tahini (sesame paste) or added to some desserts, such as helva. It has a delightful taste and tones of licorice.

NAR
(Pomegranate)

Nar is grown in several cities in Turkey, especially on the Aegean and Mediterranean coasts.

Antalya, Muğla, and Mersin are the cities with the highest production of this fruit. It can be eaten fresh or drunk as a juice. Its seeds are also used for both flavor and decoration in salads and other dishes. It is also prepared as Nar Ekşisi (pomegranate sour), a vinegar.

In Mersin, one of the cities on the Turkish Mediterranean coast, the fruits are harvested in autumn to produce Nar Ekşisi (pomegranate sour). Having been separated from the skin, the seeds are cleaned of any skin residue, and are then crushed by foot, the same way as is done in winemaking. The juice extracted from the pomegranate seeds is subsequently cooked in a pot for four hours, with the foam being skimmed off continuously. Once condensed, the syrup is set aside to cool, and salt is added. In modern times, the technique of crushing fruit by foot to extract the juice has gradually been replaced by the electric juicer, a method that reduces preparation times and is considered more suitable for home preparation.

The smell of Nar Ekşisi is intense and sweet with a bit of acidity, while its taste, in addition to being sweet and acidic, has a shiny bitter and dry aftertaste. This pomegranate sour has shiny black color, and its density is like that of heavy syrup. It is used in everyday Turkish cuisine in salads, in kısır (a dish prepared with bulgur, tomato and pepper paste) and in mercimek köftesi (lentil meatballs), as well as in dishes that require a touch of sourness.

A Green Gastronomy

Although meat and fish are important in most meals, the Turkish diet is mainly vegetable-based. Visiting a vegetable market in any corner of Turkey is a feast to the senses.

❦

There are vegetables of all colors, sizes, and textures. Options vary depending upon the region and the season. Turkish gastronomy overflows with vegetarian recipes.

Eggplant is one of their favorites. You can find it served at lunch and dinner, in appetizers, in kebabs, and whenever possible. Zucchini, green beans, tomatoes, cucumber, and all kinds of leafy, green, vegetables such as spinach (ıspanak) and purslane (semizotu), also stand out.

Vegetables are cooked in many different ways and can be served either as an accompaniment to a meat dish or as the main dish themselves.

Herbs are also consumed at all times of the day. Parsley and mint, for example, are added to a vast number of recipes. They are an essential part of the Turkish kahvaltı (breakfast), served with a wide variety of cheeses, accompanied by tomatoes and cucumber. Other herbs consumed in abundance by the Turks are leek, dill, fresh oregano, spring onions, scallions, celery, and rosemary.

Onions and garlic are used raw in salads or, in the case of garlic, mixed with yogurt as a garnish or as meze. Usually, onion and garlic are essential ingredients in sauces, soups, kebabs, and some cooked vegetable dishes, either with or without tomato sauce. The famous Adana Kebab, for example, is served with a raw onion salad, to which şumak, salt, and parsley are added.

In the same way, tubers such as potatoes, carrots, radishes and beetroots, and grains such as chickpeas and beans are all part of Turkish cuisine.

The main meat consumed in Turkey is lamb. Throughout the country it is common to see shepherds herding their sheep.

MEAT IN TURKISH CUISINE

Although chicken and beef are frequently eaten, the meat of choice for Turks is lamb. They make use of almost every part of the animal: the meat, head, brain, tongue, legs, tripe and intestines. Lamb is used in kebabs, meatballs, soups, rice dishes and also stuffed (kaburga dolması - page 120).

Dairy in Turkish Culture

Yogurt is used extensively in Turkish cuisine. Strained yogurt (suzme yogurt), with its dense texture and stronger taste than plain yogurt, is prepared by draining plain yogurt and is served as an accompaniment to some appetizers and kebabs. Yogurt is also used in the preparation of soups and sauces and in the preparation of Ayran, a popular drink in Central Asia. In Turkey, it accompanies those kebabs and dishes which are high in fat and spices.

Kaymak is a thick cream used as a breakfast spread and in delicious desserts and other dishes.

Cheeses are the main ingredient in a Turkish breakfast, in which many different types are served. They are made from cow, goat and sheep's milk. The Turks use cheese in endless savory and sweet recipes, which can be served as mezes, used as a garnish in a main dish, or to enhance some salads. They also constitute the main stuffing for some 'börek' (puff pastry) recipes.

Beyaz peynir (White cheese), similar to feta, is the Turks' favorite and is present in many mezes, salads and desserts. The Marmara region is renowned for its production of white cheese. A matured version of this type of cheese, eski kaşar (old kaşar), is produced in the mountainous areas of Kars, in the northeast of the country.

Hünkar Beğendi (the Sultan's favorite – page 140), a mouthwatering dish prepared with an eggplant béchamel complemented by stewed meat, includes kaşar cheese as one of its main ingredients. Kaşar is an unaged cheese with a mild flavor and firm texture. It is also used on top of pizzas and in toasted sandwiches. Along the same lines is Dil cheese, a soft cheese with a very delicate flavor eaten at breakfast and in various types of sandwiches.

Tulum cheese is made with both goat and sheep's milk. It is a strong, pungent cheese, mainly used in dishes where the taste of the cheese must predominate.

In Turkey, there are also regional cheeses whose flavor and texture change depending on the ingredients present in the region and the climate. Some of these cheeses have spices and herbs added to them, thus increasing their complexity.

CEREALS IN TURKISH CUISINE

Wheat is another essential component of Turkish cuisine. From it come bulgur and flour and then bread. Most dishes eaten in Turkey contain flour in one form or another.

Bread, often served during religious celebrations, is a mealtime staple. It is served at breakfast but also as an accompaniment to practically any type of kebab. Bread is prepared with and without yeast and comes in many shapes and sizes, balls, squares, baguettes, small, and large loaves.

Such is the importance of bread in Turkish cuisine that during the strictest lockdown implemented by the government during the COVİD-19 pandemic, bakeries were one of the few businesses with permission to remain open and sell their products.

A quintessential household staple is simit, a salty bread that resembles brown donuts sprinkled with sesame seeds. It is sold in bakeries, supermarkets, and hot from small roadside stalls across the country.

The famous **Yufka dough** (filo pastry) is also made with flour and is the main ingredient in such famous dishes as baklava and böreks, amongst numerous other recipes.

Kadayıf is a tiny pasta, a bit like vermicelli, prepared with flour and water and fed through a machine with a strainer on a very hot rolling tray. It is the main ingredient of famous Turkish desserts such as Künefe (page 161), and the dessert that also bears its name, Kadayıf (page 160), originally from Hatay (page 143). It can also be used in savory dishes.

Rice also plays an essential role in Turkish cuisine, where it is served both sweet and savory. It is served with meat, in soups and in numerous delicious recipes.

ÇAY

(Turkish Tea)

Black tea is one of the most consumed products in the entire country. The tea-drinking tradition in Turkey can be considered as sacred.

Tea is served throughout the day and without a need for an excuse. It is taken by young and old alike. It is served morning, noon and night and it's always offered by the Turks at both formal and informal meetings.

When haggling in the stores and markets, a cup of tea is always offered. Restaurants traditionally serve this hot and intensely flavored liquid to help with digestion at the end of a meal. It is always present in the Turkish kahvaltı (breakfast).

The offering of çay is a symbolic gesture, a symbol of acceptance, sympathy, respect and consideration.

Delicious Çay

Kahvaltı in Ulus – Ankara

Kokoreç

KAHVALTI
(Turkish breakfast)

It is well known that breakfast is the most important meal of the day. For the Turks, this is an understatement. Kahvaltı is a complete gastronomic feast which ensures that you start the day full of energy.

It consists of various cheeses, eggs prepared in different ways, and sauces such as muhammara. Vegetables and greens such as arugula, cucumber, tomatoes, parsley, and assorted peppers, cooked or raw, can also be found in the Turkish breakfast.

A selection of dry fruits, jams, honey, butter and kaymak is also served, along with bread which is usually hot and crispy. Çay is the one unwavering element at breakfast, while Turkish kahve (coffee) is optional.

Menemen, a delicious mixture of eggs, tomato, and chili, is another option.

Depending on the region, some additional ingredients are added.

STREET FOOD

Kokoreç is a typical Turkish street food consisting of roasted lamb intestines, seasoned with various herbs, and which is usually cooked in a rotisserie. These intestines are served as bread stuffing and heated in a pan with the fat leftover from preparing the Kokoreç.

Kokoreç stalls are to be found in markets and, at night, in entertainment areas. Its vendors usually put on a real spectacle, using their utensils, such as the knives with which they cut the intestines, as instruments with which to play a very particular and unique form of music.

COOKWARES
AND UTENSILS

Zirh

With a few modifications, the vast majority of tools used in Turkish cooking today have been inherited from the Turks' ancestors.

The use of pans and copper items, clay pots, knives and skewers for their many kebabs, as well as the ovens in which they still bake their bread, all relate back to the passage of some ancient civilization through the lands of Anatolia.

The stone oven in which modern-day Turks bake breads, pizzas and kebabs, uses a technique similar to that used by the nomadic immigrants from Central Asia with their **tandoor**. As in ancient times, copper pots or imitations of them are still used to serve traditional dishes. The **Menemen** (see recipe on page 88), a mouthwatering mixture of eggs, tomatoes and chilies, is served on a copper plate similar to those used hundreds of years ago.

In Anatolia, since the time of the **Seljuks**, iron has been forged into swords with which they used to fight their continuous battles. Over the years this expertise evolved into making utensils for daily use. One of the instruments that still persists is the **Zırh**, a large knife used to cut meat, mainly for kebabs. Its use in Turkey requires prior training, since it can be dangerous in inexperienced hands. It is a heavy, crescent-shaped knife that is usually handled with both hands. **Zırh**-cut meat, when prepared for kebabs like the Adana, results in thin, almost millimeter-wide slivers, allowing for better texture and cooking.

Another historical tool that is commonly used today is the **Saç**, a kind of wok-style pan generally used to cook meat, vegetables and their famous **Gözleme** (see recipe on page 87). You can find these pans made of copper or imitation copper in craft markets and they are also used as large serving dishes.

The **sobah** is a wood-burning metal stove used to keep houses warm in winter. In some family restaurants, the heat of the sobah is used to heat the bread and to keep the **çay** warm. The **Dolma oyacağı** is used to core vegetables prior to filling them (see dolma). The **Dolma taşı** is a clay lid with holes. It is used to cover and compress the dolmas during the cooking process.

Oklava is a small rolling pin widely used in Turkish cuisine. Of much smaller diameter than the one commonly known in the West, the oklava is the main instrument to prepare most of the Turkish dishes that include dough, including their famous baklava and hundreds of other recipes.

From top to bottom:
Bakir Ayran Bardak
Dolma Oyacağı
Eski Kevgir
Antique Turkish cookware
Dolma Taşı
Oklava (object on the right)

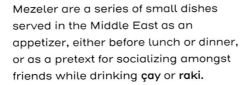

MEZELER

(Appetizer)

Mezeler are a series of small dishes served in the Middle East as an appetizer, either before lunch or dinner, or as a pretext for socializing amongst friends while drinking **çay** or **raki**.

In Turkey, mezes vary depending on the region. In the **Black Sea Region** (page 133), mezes are usually made up of seafood (anchovies, shrimps, fish, octopus). By contrast, in **Gaziantep** (page 105), closer to the Syrian border, mezes traditionally contain olives, dried fruits, and pistachio nuts. Gaziantep is one of the foremost pistachio producers in Turkey, and their nuts are exported worldwide, due to their high quality.

In **Mardin** (page 105), mezes are usually prepared with sour fruit, such as green plums. Despite regional variations, suzme yogurt, eggplant, mint, dill, pomegranate, and chili are the key ingredients generally found in mezes throughout the country.

MEZE
RECIPES

COOKING WITH SERPIL AND SEVGI KARAHAN

- Mezeler

Serpil and Sevgi are two excellent cooks who are very proud of their gastronomic heritage. The first time they invited us to their home, they prepared a table full of mezes. It was an excellent arrangement of colors, flavors, and textures, presented with such majesty that it was impossible not to notice it. We spent the entire dinner talking about food. I asked them for recipes and techniques, and they, happy and proud, answered all my questions. At that moment, I decided that something so well achieved should be shared with the world. I invited them to be part of this project, and they immediately accepted.

❝ My interest in cooking started in childhood. I always watched my mother. I baked my first cookie alone at the age of 6. I've always loved trying different flavors. I started doing this job professionally during my university years. I took training courses and attended several workshops. I worked in the kitchens of various hotels. It's a job I love to do. The Central Anatolia Region has a rich cuisine. It is possible to find diversity, different flavors and dishes suitable for all different tastes not only in this region but in all regions. Turkey has a cuisine that fascinates everyone.

Serpil Karahan.

❝ Cooking and the presentation of the food I cook are very important to me. I did not receive much professional training. I mostly like to cook Eastern Anatolian dishes and kebabs. I think there is no dish in Turkish cuisine that I cannot cook and do not know. Cooking is a great passion of mine. I love to cook different local dishes by going to that region and learning from the master.

Sevgi Karahan

YAPRAK SARMASI

(Stuffed vine leaves)

Serves 6-8

Ingredients
500g vine leaves in brine

For the stuffing
2 medium onions
100ml vegetable oil
200g rice
1 tsp black pepper
1 tsp toz pul biber (red pepper powdered) (see page 26)
1 tsp acı pul biber (powdered red chili pepper) (see page 26)
1 tsp cumin
1 tsp dried mint
1 bunch of parsley
1 tsp salt

For assembling the rolls
1 lemon cut into wedges
2 tbsp olive oil
Zest of lemon

For the dough:
Step 1: Drain the vine leaves in brine, rinse, and cover with hot water. Leave for 2 minutes and then drain.

Preparing the stuffing
Step 2: Grate the onions with a cheese grater and mix them with the vegetable oil. Wash the rice and add to the onions. Add the spices, finely chopped parsley and salt. Mix well to integrate all the ingredients.

Assembling your sarma
Step 3: Place some of the stuffing onto the widest part of a leaf and roll, closing on both sides to prevent the filling from spilling during cooking. Repeat.

Step 4: Transfer your rolls to the bottom of a pot and add some lemon wedges. Cover the rolls with an upside-down plate on top to prevent them from splitting during cooking.

Step 5: Pour 5 cups of water and two tablespoons of olive oil onto the plate and let them simmer for an hour. Garnish with lemon zest.

ATOM

Serves 6

Ingredients
2 eggplants
1 garlic clove
Salt to taste
4 tbsp strained yogurt (see page 37)
1 tbsp olive oil
6–8 dried red chili peppers
1 tbsp butter

Step 1: Prick small holes all over your eggplants with the tip of a sharp knife and grill them over a high heat. Peel and remove the skin. Crush to make puree.

Step 2: Grate the garlic and add it to the eggplant puree. Add salt and strained yogurt and mix the ingredients. Transfer to your presentation plate.

Step 3: In a frying pan, sauté the dried red chilies in olive oil for two minutes. Add the butter and cook until foamy. Pour over the eggplant paste.

℘ATLICAN SÖĞÜRME

(Spitting eggplants)

Serves 6-8

Ingredients
2 onions
4 tomatoes
2 garlic cloves
2 green peppers, roasted
2 long black eggplants
2 capia peppers
olive oil
1 tsp salt

You will need:
Plastic film

Step 1: Chop the onion, tomatoes, garlic, and green chili into small pieces. Set aside.

Step 2: Roast the eggplants and capia peppers until soft. Wrap in plastic film and let them rest until cool. Peel and remove the skin. Dice and set aside.

Step 3: In a frying pan, heat the oil over medium heat. Add the onion and cook until it turns translucent. Add the tomatoes, garlic, and diced green peppers and cook for 5 minutes. Add the eggplants, capia pepper and salt and cook for an additional two minutes. Serve hot.

LEVREK MARIN

(Marinated seabass)

Serves 6

Ingredients
300 gr sea bass fillets
1 onion

For the sauce
juice of 1 lime
juice of 1 orange
1 tbsp granulated sugar
1 tsp black pepper
3 tbsp olive oil
2 bay leaves
zest of 1 orange
1 tbsp mustard
1 tsp salt

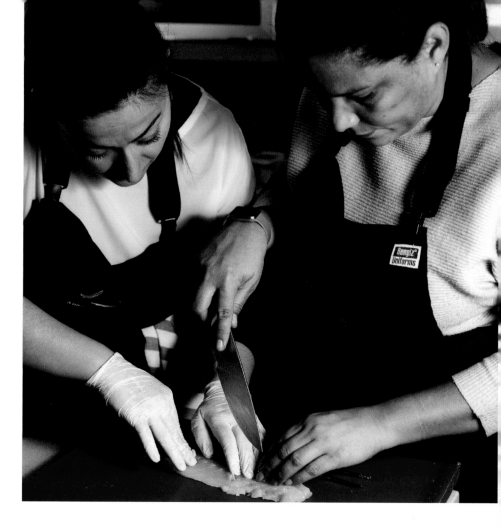

Step 1: Remove any bones that the fish may have and cut into approximately 2x2cm cubes.

Step 2: Cut the onion into very fine julienne strips. Place them in a bowl and mix with the cubed fish. Set aside.

For the sauce

Step 3: Mix the lime and orange juice, sugar, black pepper, olive oil, bay leaves, orange zest, mustard, and salt in a bowl. Mix well and cover the fish with this sauce. Let the fish marinate overnight before serving so that it absorbs the sauce. Serve cold.

YOĞURTLU SEMIZOTU

(Purslane with yogurt)

Serves 4

Ingredients
1 bunch purslane
1 cup of plain yogurt
2 tbsp strained yogurt
2 tbsp olive oil
1 tsp salt
1 clove of garlic
*5–6 walnuts coarsely
chopped*

To garnish
Olive oil
Chopped walnuts
Red chili powder

Step 1: Wash the purslane in plenty of water. Separate the leaves one by one with your hands, being careful not to tear them. Strain and discard the stems. Place them in a bowl and set them aside.

Step 2: Place the yogurts, olive oil, and salt in a bowl. Grate the garlic clove and add it to the bowl. Whisk until smooth. Add the chopped walnuts and mix.

Step 3: Stir the purslane into the yogurt mix until all the ingredients are fully combined. Serve this salad by sprinkling a little olive oil, walnuts, and a little chili powder on top.

HAMSI TAVA
(Anchovies in the pan)

Serves 6-8

Ingredients
500 gr boneless anchovies
Salt to taste
200 gr corn flour
2 tbsp vegetable oil

To garnish
A lemon cut into slices
A radish cut into slices

Step 1: Sprinkle the anchovies with salt and then coat them entirely with corn flour.

Step 2: Using a kitchen brush, cover the bottom of a pan with oil. Cover the bottom of the pan with the fish and cook for 8 minutes, or until the underside of the fish is golden brown.

Step 3: Using a flat plate or lid for support, turn the cake upside-down to allow it to cook evenly on both sides.

Step 4: When both sides of the fish are browned, transfer to the serving plate. Garnish with lemon and radish slices.

Turkish Muhammara

Serves 6-8

Ingredients
3 tbsp tomato paste
3 tbsp red pepper paste
1/2 cup olive oil
6 cloves garlic (crushed)
2 tsp cumin
2 tsp paprika
1 cup breadcrumbs
1 cup chopped walnuts

Step 1: Transfer all the ingredients to a hand processor and blend until completely combined. Serve and garnish with some chopped walnuts.

Note: Although in its original version the Muhammara is served spread in a plate with the walnuts on top, Serpil and Sevgi present it by shaping it into croquettes with their hands.

HUMMUS *(Alicia's recipe)*

Serves 6-8

Ingredients
300g softened chickpeas
3 tbsp tahini (sesame paste)
3 tbsp lemon juice
2 cloves garlic
1 tsp red pepper flakes
coriander leaves for decoration
Salt to taste

Step 1: Place all the ingredients into a food processor and blend until obtaining a fluid, lump-free cream.

Step 2: Sprinkle with red pepper flakes and garnish with some coriander leaves. Serve with fresh vegetables, crackers or lavaş (page 90).

Tip: For a more fluid hummus, add three tablespoons of the water from cooking the chickpeas or room temperature water and mix well.

You should know: In Turkey, it is common to serve hot hummus, with some slices of Pastirma (dried meat– page 90) on top.

KADAYIFLI KARIDES

(Shrimps with kadayıf)

Serves 5

Ingredients
For the shrimps
10 jumbo shrimp
200g kadayıf strips (see page 38)
1 tsp red chili pepper, powdered
1 tsp salt
50ml olive oil
Enough vegetable oil to deep-fry.
For the dipping sauce (Alicia's recipe)
1/2 cup rice vinegar
1 1/2 tbsp salt
1/4 cup garlic, chopped
1 1/2 cups water
1 cup white sugar
1 tbsp fresh Thai red chilies, diced

For the shrimp
Step 1: Wash the shrimp and remove the head and intestines. Peel them, separate the tail. Set aside.

Step 2: Spread the kadayıf strips on a tray and sprinkle them with red chili pepper powder and salt. Pour in the olive oil and mix well to soften the kadayıf strips by integrating the salt and chili powder.

Step 3: Roll the cleaned shrimp with the kadayıf strips and press with your hands to compact.

Step 4: Fry the shrimp in plenty of oil until they begin to brown. Remove from the pan and place them on absorbent kitchen paper to remove excess fat.

For the sauce
Step 5: Add vinegar, salt, garlic, and water to a small saucepan. Bring to a boil. Add the sugar and fresh chilies, reduce the heat to a minimum and cook for 15 minutes. Remove from heat and let cool. Blend it and serve it with your shrimp.

ﬄHTAPOT SALATASI

(Octopus salad - Alicia's recipe)

Serves 6-8

Ingredients
1 yellow onion
1 small bunch parsley
1 small thyme sprig
2 bay leaves
3 garlic cloves
1 carrot
500g octopus
1 whole potato

For the garnish
1 red onion
¼ cup vinegar
2 garlic cloves
1 tbsp vegetable oil
5ml olive oil
Salt to taste
a handful of parsley leaves

Step 1: Place two liters of water in a large pot. Add the yellow onion cut in half and unpeeled. Make a bouquet garni with the herbs and place it into the pot. Crush the garlic cloves with the flat of a knife and add to the pot. Add the carrot cut in half lengthwise. Put the pot on a high heat and bring it to a boil.

Step 2: Wash the octopus under plenty of running water. When the broth in the pot begins to boil, 'scare' the octopus by dipping it into the boiling broth and immediately scooping it out 5 or 6 times. These sudden temperature changes will allow the collagen in the octopus flesh to break down, it will yield a more tender octopus.

Add a whole potato to the pot and cook the octopus until the potato is fully cooked (about 25 minutes). Remove the octopus from the pot and leave to cool.

Step 3: Julienne the red onion and soak in vinegar for 20 minutes. Chop the garlic. Sauté together with the onion in the vegetable oil. Set aside.

Step 4: Clean the octopus by removing the skin, the inside of the head, and the mouth. Cut into slices about 2cm wide. Transfer to a bowl and cover with the olive oil, the precooked onions, and salt. Mix and chill until serving. Serve with some parsley leaves.

HAYDARI

Serves 6

Ingredients
1 tbsp butter
1 tsp dried mint
6 tbsp strained yogurt
100 gr white or feta cheese
(see page 37)
A few sprigs dill
2 garlic cloves
Salt to taste

For the garnish
Orange slices
Mint leaves

Step 1: Melt the butter in a pan and add the powdered mint until it starts to froth. Remove from the heat and let cool.

Step 2: Place the yogurt in a bowl. Crush the white cheese and add to the yogurt. Very finely chop the dill and grate the garlic and add to the bowl. Add the previously fried mint along with the salt. Mix and serve with a splash of olive oil and a few sprigs of dill or some leaves of fresh mint.

KEREVIZ SALATA
(Celery roots salad)

Serves 6-8

Ingredients
2 large celery roots
300ml strained yogurt (see page 37)
2 garlic cloves – grated
Salt to taste

For the garnish
Orange slices
Mint leaves

Step 1: Grate the celery root with a cheese grater and mix well with the yogurt, grated garlic, and salt. Serve over orange slices and garnish with some fresh mint leaves.

Turkish Recipes by Region

Central Anatolia

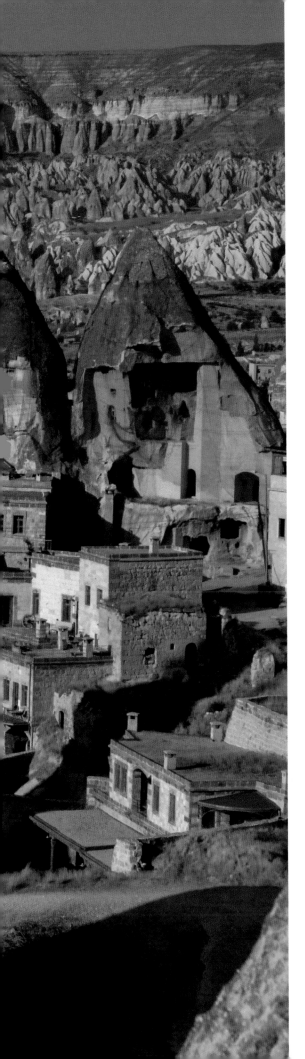

A region that, as its name implies, is located in the center of the country. Cities as important as **Ankara**, the administrative capital of Turkey since 1923 and seat of the presidency of the republic and the main ministries, as well as diplomatic delegations are in this region.

Another city in Central Anatolia is **Konya**. Because of its religious importance to Muslims, Konya is considered one of the most conservative cities in Turkey, where it has come to be called the citadel of Islam. This city was one of those visited by Saint Paul the Apostle in Turkey. Yalal ad-Din Muhammad Rumi, a mystical poet, also known as Mevlana, died and was buried in this city. After his death, his followers founded the Sufi order of Mevleví, which has as a particularity the meditation of the whirling dervishes, which is carried out through a constant circular movement and has become a great attraction to both national and international tourists.

Occupying 19% of the Turkish territory, the climate in the region is dry-continental, with very cold winters characterized by heavy and long-lasting snowfalls and hot and arid summers. Its height above sea-level varies between 600 to 1200 meters.

Given the aridity of the terrain, plantations in this region are only to be found close to rivers, where the valleys are wide enough. Nevertheless, one-third of the total wheat and barley cultivated in Turkey is grown in this region. Similarly, potatoes, lentils, and chickpeas are cultivated. Another source of income in the region is rug weaving, especially in cities such as Konya, Kayseri and Sivas.

Of touristic and historical significance **Kapadokya** is also located in the region, characterized by its emblematic caverns that were formed, among other natural events, by magma following the eruption of several volcanoes, including Mount Erciyes. Due to the particularity of its landscapes, unique in the world, Kapadokya was recognized by UNESCO in 1985 and is protected as a World Heritage Site.

Ulus – Altındağ – Ankara

ANKARA: DISCOVERING ULUS

We started by exploring Ulus, the old part of Ankara where the city's castle is located and, since then, my favorite corner of the whole country.

My eyes marveled at the warm hues of the neighborhood's walls and rooftops, an all-enveloping combination of ochre and crimson. A landscape of streets and walls forged by so much history.

Ulus was, for me, a complete revelation. I was struck by the intense smell of its spices: cumin, sumac, turmeric. The combination of textures of its nuts, walnuts, pistachios, almonds, and dried seeds in varieties unimagined by me until that moment. The intense colors of the spices and dried vegetables laid out on the sidewalks.

And its people; the people of Ulus, with an ancient and wise glance in their eyes. They became my family, my touristic guides and gastronomic advisers. With them, I quickly learned, even without speaking their language, all about that unique rich combination of eggs, chili peppers, and tomatoes that the Turks call **Menemen** (page 88). I encountered those delicious crêpes filled with eggplant or cheese or whatever you can imagine, called **Gözleme** (page 87), and I warmed my soul in winter, drinking that delicious hot and cinnamon-flavored milky drink called Sahlep. I sat down with them to drink Çay (Turkish tea) in front of a Soba, the traditional wood-burning stove used for heating (and warming bread).

I walked through its narrow streets. I immersed myself in its markets. There was an unforgettable one selling vegetables and fish with that smell that intensifies with every step you take and with a range of textures and colors that, for me, can only compare to the sensation of entering an amusement park. It is impossible to list the colors and variety of its herbs and fruits, garden-fresh and inviting. I often went just to let my eyes wander through that rainbow of aromas, colors, and flavors and to see the people who call at you, always smiling, showing their fresh product.

Ulus was my gateway into Turkish gastronomy. In its streets, I discovered an entirely new universe of flavors, smells, and textures. The kindness and authenticity of its people motivated me to try harder to discover the hidden secrets of this beautiful country, and that is how this gastronomic journey began.

I started traveling and getting to know each hidden corner of Turkey, and the more I traveled, the more I wanted to know. Every Turk I met received me in the same way; with sincere kindness, a full heart, and a raw goodness that was unknown to me until then.

Cooking with Semra Ersoy

- Ankara

Semra is a woman with a strong character and a lovely soul. She was my right hand in my restaurant in Turkey and my most direct source of information when I tried to create new recipes to attract customers as demanding as the Turkish. Thanks to her, I fell in love with baby okra and tarhana çorba. She also taught me how to do things in a more simple and practical way. She had a passion for plating food and was always avid to learn new techniques, which made me admire and respect her even more.

❝ I was born in Istanbul in 1976 but I have lived most of my life in Ankara. I'm married and the mother of two kids. I started cooking when my first child was born, improving myself by doing extensive research on pastries and baking. Vegetable and meat dishes are the types that I like to cook the most."

Semra Ersoy

TOZ TARHANA ÇORBASI

(Powdered tarhana soup)

Serves 6

Ingredients
1kg tomatoes
1kg onions
1kg red peppers
500g green peppers
1 small handful of parsley
1 sprig of dill
1 handful of fresh mint
1/2 kg boiled chickpeas
1kg suzme yogurt
2 tbsp salt
2.5kg flour

Step 1: Cut the tomatoes, onion, and peppers into wedges and bring them to a boil in a deep pot making sure to cover them with enough water. Add the herbs and cook for about two hours or until they are all very soft.

Step 2: Add the cooked chickpeas and blend. Pass the mixture through a fine strainer and discard the remains.

Step 3: Add the yogurt and salt to the mixture. Separate 1 kg of the flour and add it to mix of yogurt little by little, until all the ingredients are well mixed. The result should be a dense dough that sticks to the fingers but is not runny. Set aside the rest of the flour to be used in the following days.

Step 4: Put the dough in a bowl and cover it with a clean towel. Leave it to rest for 6–7 days. The longer you wait, the sourer it will be. Mix the dough in the morning, noon and evening every day. If it is too watery, add flour until it has the consistency of pancake batter.

Step 5: When enough time has passed, divide it into small pieces on an oven tray covered with parchment paper. Place them in a spot where there's indirect sunlight (never direct), so that they dry in the air. Let it dry completely. Note that the drying process could take a few days, depending on the weather.

Step 6: Blend and strain the Tarhana once more until powdered. Store in a hermetically sealed glass jar, until needed. See the following recipe to prepare Tarhana soup.

Tarhana is a dried fermented soup prepared during the summer, when the vegetables are perfect. Tomato, pepper, onion and herbs are cooked until softened and then allowed to dry under the sun. This powdered soup lasts for months and is conserved to be prepared later, during the cold winters.

Preparing the
TARHANA ÇORBA

Serves 4

Ingredients
2 garlic cloves – pounded
3 tbsp vegetable oil
1 tbsp tomato paste
1 lt. of lukewarm vegetable stock
4 tbsp dried Tarhana çorba
Salt to taste

Step 1: Sauté the garlic cloves with vegetable oil in a heavy-bottomed pot for about 30 seconds. Add the tomato paste and mix well. Sauté for approximately two minutes. Dilute with 1/4 litre of vegetable stock.

Step 2: In separate bowl, mix the tarhana powder with the rest of the vegetable stock and whisk until there are no lumps. Add this mixture to the pot and cook while stirring until the soup begins to boil. Add salt to taste and serve hot.

BAMYA ETLI
(Okra with meat)

Serves 4

Ingredients
500g baby okra
3 tbsp olive oil
300g beef – diced
1 medium onion – diced
1 garlic clove – diced
1 tbsp tomato paste
1 tomato – diced
1 tsp salt
1 tsp black pepper
Juice of half lemon

Step 1: Wash the okra well and dry. Peel the thickest part of the stem. Set aside.

Step 2: Heat the oil in a pot and add the meat. Mix well to seal on all sides. Add the onions and garlic and cook for two minutes. Add the tomato paste, sauté, and add the water. Let cook for approximately 10 minutes.

Step 3: Add the okra, salt, pepper, and lemon juice to the pot. Move and cook over medium heat for 30 minutes.

In Turkish cuisine, Bamya (okra) is used when the vegetable is still very small. That's the reason why it has such a delicate taste and texture. İn this recipe, the combination of the okra and the diced beef result in a mouthwatering and light dish.

COOKING WITH NURHAN GÖNÜLALAN

- Kayserı

Nurhan made me fall in love with Menemem (p. 88). She has a small and authentic restaurant called Gonulalan Mantı Evi. It's in Ulus, the oldest area of Ankara and where the city's castle is located. Every day, she prepares delicious recipes, which, despite their simplicity, overflow with flavor. We exchanged recipes and tips despite her almost total ignorance of English and my limited Turkish. With her, I learned the secrets of the Sahlep and the Gözleme. There I could also appreciate the abysmal difference between bread toasted with modern techniques and bread toasted under the heat of the burning coals of a Sobah. Thanks to her, I got to know tepsi matısı, tasty baked ravioli, originally from Kayseri, her hometown. Every Friday, I looked for new excuses to go to Ulus to eat Menemem while enjoying her company and her lively restaurant.

❝ I was curious at a very young age. I was 10 years old when I started in the kitchen. I used to make cookies. The ladies in my neighborhood used to call me to help to roll the leaves for the Yaprak Sarmasi. Then, after a year or two, I was able to cook almost any dish. I would end up next to whoever was cooking, and I would pay attention and find out how to prepare the dishes by myself. I like to make cookies the most, but my job was to prepare the Mantı."

Nurhan Gönülalan

CLASSIC MANTI

(Small ravioli - Classic recipe)

Serves 6

Ingredients
For the Mantı dough
3 cups flour
A pinch of salt
1 egg
1 cup water

For the stuffing
1 large onion
300g minced meat
Salt and pepper
1 tsp red pepper

For the sauce
2 tbsp butter
1 tbsp tomato paste
A pinch of salt

For the garnish
2 garlic cloves
1 cup plain yogurt
1/4 cup water
Şumak or red pepper to taste

For the dough
Step 1: Mix the flour with a pinch of salt and place it on a clean, flat surface.

Step 2: Add the egg and half of the water in the center and begin to mix, adding the rest of the water little by little. Knead the dough until you get a homogeneous mixture. The dough must be elastic and must not stick to the fingers. Divide into three equal parts and leave to rest covered with a clean cloth for a few minutes while you prepare the meat.

For the stuffing
Step 3: Grate the onion and mix it with the meat. Add salt, pepper, and red pepper and mix well, kneading with your hands until you get a compact mixture.

Preparing your ravioli
Step 4: Roll out the dough using a thin rolling pin and cut it into small squares of about 2x2cm. Put a small portion of the meat mixture onto the center of each square and close it by joining the four corners in the center of the mantı.

Step 5: In a pot of boiling water, cook your ravioli for approximately 15 minutes. Drain them and have them ready for the next step.

Preparing the sauce
Step 6: In a heavy-bottomed skillet, melt your butter over medium heat. Add the tomato sauce and sauté for two minutes. Add a pinch of salt and ¼ cup of water to dissolve the sauce. Strain the mantı and add them to the sauce. Let them cook for 5 more minutes.

Preparing the yogurt garnish
Step 7: Grate the garlic cloves and mix them with the yogurt and water. Set aside.

Plating your Mantı
Step 8: Serve your mantı in deep plates. Place the yogurt and garlic mixture on top and sprinkle with mint and şumak or red pepper.

TEPSI MANTISI
(Tray ravioli)

Serves 6

Ingredients: same used for Manti recipe.
Repeat steps 1, 2, and 3 from the previous recipe (Manti)

Step 4: Instead of cutting the dough into squares, cut strips of about 3x50 cm. Distribute the meat mixture in small portions over the dough, separated from each other by about 2 cm. Press the empty part of the dough with your fingers to create a chain of small meat pockets. Cut each meat pocket symmetrically with the help of a knife. Carefully place them on a round oven tray.

Step 5: In a heavy-bottomed skillet, melt your butter over medium heat. Add the tomato sauce and the salt and sauté for two minutes. Add 2 cups of hot water to dissolve the sauce. Place the sauce on top of your ravioli and bake them at 180 degrees Celsius for 20-25 minutes.

Step 6: Grate the garlic, mix it with the yogurt and water, and place it over your mantı.

Plating your Mantı

Step 7: Sprinkle a little red chili powder.

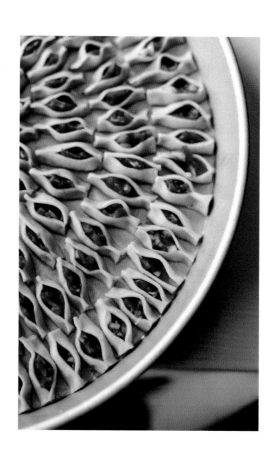

YALANCI MANTI
(Fake raviolii)

Serves 6

Repeat steps 1, 2 and 3.
With the same ingredients for the previous recipe.

Step 4: In a skillet, sauté the onion with 2 tbsp of olive oil until translucent. Add the meat, mix, and cook well for two or three minutes. Then add 1 tbsp of tomato paste, salt, pepper, and mix well. Pour in 1/4 cup of hot water, stirring until the sauce dissolves. Let it cook for 5 minutes. Take off heat and set aside.

Step 5: Instead of cutting the dough into squares, cut strips of about 3x50 cm which are then to be cut into triangles. In a pot of boiling water, cook your ravioli for approximately 15 minutes. Drain and serve it in a deep dish. Add a little of the yogurt sauce and meat on top. Sprinkle with parsley to garnish.

GÖZLEME

(Turkish stuffed crepes)

Serves 12 crepes

For the dough
2 cups warm water
1 tsp sugar
1 tbsp dry yeast
2 tsp salt
6 cups flour

For the stuffing
1/2 bunch parsley
250g goat cheese (semi-skimmed white cheese upon request)
1/2 bunch parsley

For serving
1 tbsp butter

Step 1: Mix the warm water with the sugar and yeast and let it rest for 10 minutes.

Step 2: Mix the salt with the flour in a bowl. Add the yeast mixture little by little and mix well. Knead for a few minutes until you get an elastic and homogeneous dough. Divide equally the dough into balls of 60 gr and place them on a tray. Cover with a cloth and leave to rest for 10 minutes.

Step 3: Finely chop the parsley and mix with the goat cheese.

Step 4: With the help of a rolling pin, rollout the dough in circles of approximately 24 cm. Place 3 or 4 tablespoons of cheese filling in the center of each circle and fold the Gözleme over into semi-circles, pressing the edges together with your fingers to prevent them from opening during cooking.

Step 5: Cook your Gözleme for two minutes on each side, or until light golden brown. Serve hot, with a bit of butter.

Note: This Gözleme recipe is straightforward to prepare. It is ideal for preparing breakfast or a quick snack. You can prepare it with as many fillings as your imagination allows.

MENEMEN

Serves 2

Ingredients
3 ripe tomatoes
1 medium onion
3 long green chilies
2 tsp vegetable oil
2 tbsp butter
Salt
2 eggs
Red chili pepper powder
as desired
Some parsley leaves

Step 1: Peel the tomatoes and dice them. Dice the onion into small cubes. Finely chop the green peppers. Set aside.

Step 2: In a heavy-bottomed pan, heat the oil and butter until the latter melts. Add the onion and sauté until translucent. Add the green chili and cook for about two minutes. Add the tomato. When the tomatoes begin to release their juice, add the salt.

Step 3: Add the eggs to the pan and mix lightly. Once the eggs are cooked, remove the menemen from the heat.

Step 4: Sprinkle with spicy red chili pepper and parsley if desired.

TESTI KEBAB
(Clay pottery kebab)

Serves 6

Ingredients
For the kebab
1kg beef
3 big onions
12 garlic cloves
6 long green peppers
6 ripe tomatoes
6 long green peppers
1 tbsp brown sugar
1 cup vegetable oil
1 tbsp salt
1 tbsp spicy red pepper
1 tbsp oregano
1 tbsp brown sugar
6 bay leaves
1 ½ cups beef stock

For covering the pot
Aluminum paper
200g bread dough

You also will need
6 clay pots

Step 1: Preheat your oven to 180°C.

Step 2: Cut the meat and vegetables into 2x2cm squares. Set aside.

Assembling your pottery kebab
Step 3: In your well-cleaned clay pottery, start by adding a tablespoon of oil to each one. In turn, place the rest of the ingredients starting with the meat, then onion, garlic, chili peppers, tomatoes, sugar, salt, and spices. Cover by pouring ¼ cup of beef stock into each jar and finally add a second tablespoon of oil.

Step 4: Cover the opening of each jar with aluminum foil and shake vigorously to mix the ingredients inside. Cover the foil with bread dough. Use a toothpick to make a small hole to let the steam escape during cooking.

Step 5: Put the pots in the oven and cook for 2 hours, rotating them every half hour to ensure that everything cooks evenly.

Step 6: Serve your kebabs hot with bread and salad.

Note: In Cappadocia, restaurants traditionally break the pot in front of the diners when serving testi kebabs, hitting them on the edge of the bread. The kebab is then served in the same broken pot.

LAVAŞ

(Turkish Bread)

Serves 5

Ingredients
For 5 loaves of bread
300g flour
200ml lukewarm water
1 tsp salt
1 tsp sugar
6g yeast

Step 1: Preheat your oven to 200 °C.

Step 2: Place the flour in a bowl and mix with salt.

Step 3: Mix the warm water with sugar and add the yeast. Leave it to ferment for 10 minutes.

Step 4: Mix the dry ingredients with the liquids and knead for about 4-5 minutes or until you get an elastic and smooth dough that does not stick to your hands.

Step 5: Roll out the dough. Fold it up and roll it out again and divide into 5 equal parts. Roll each small piece of dough out again and then fold and roll it again, first lengthwise and then widthwise to add air to the dough. Once finished divide it into 5 balls.

Step 6: Roll out each ball of dough again, creating a very flat, circular shape. Eliminate the excess flour and bake it in your preheated oven for 5-6 minutes.

İÇLI KÖFTE
(stuffed meatballs)

Makes 50

Ingredients
For the dough
4 cups fine bulgur
4+1 cups water
4 eggs
4 cups flour
2 tsp salt

For the stuffing
1 tbsp butter
1/4 cup vegetable oil
2 medium onions – diced
2kg potatoes
2 tsp salt
1 tsp cumin
1 tsp black pepper
1 tsp spicy red pepper

For garnishing
2 tbsp butter
2 tsp pul biber (red chili pepper powder)

Preparing the dough
Step 1: In a bowl, mix the 4 cups of bulgur with 4 cups of water. Cover with a clean cloth and let it rest for 20 minutes.

Step 2: Add 4 eggs, flour, salt, and the remaining cup of water to the bulgur. Mix to form a dough that does not stick to your fingers. Set aside.

Preparing the stuffing
Step 3: Boil the potatoes until soft. Puree them and add the cooked onions. Add salt and spices and mix well to form a compact dough. Set aside.

Step 4: Add 4 eggs, flour, salt, and a cup of water to the bulgur. Mix to form a dough that does not stick to your fingers.

Assembling the Köfte
Step 5: Wet your hands and form balls with the bulgur dough. Make a hole in the center, supporting yourself with your fingers, and fill with a little of the potato dough. Close the balls carefully, preventing the filling from coming out, and press lightly to shape it into a mandarine orange (clementine) shape.

Step 6: Add a pinch of salt to a deep pot of boiling water. Add your köfte and cook for 10 minutes.

For garnishing
Step 7: Melt two tablespoons of butter and add 2 teaspoons of powdered paprika. Sauté for a few seconds and spread over your köfte.

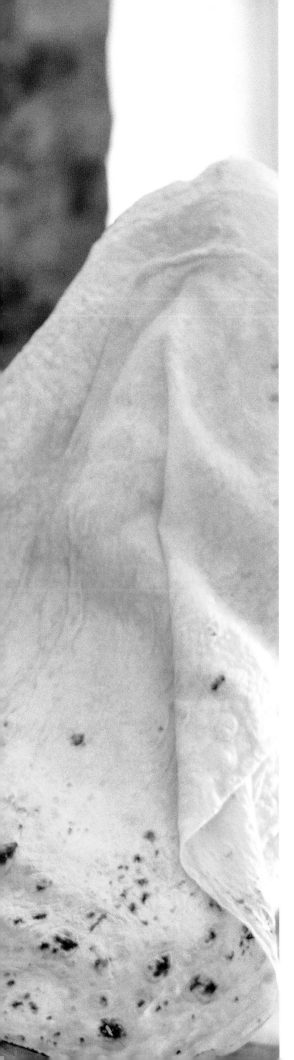

EASTERN ANATOLIA

Northern Region

Sharing borders with countries such as İran, Azerbaijan, Armenia and Georgia, the Eastern region of Turkey is characterized by its impressive mountains and archaeological ruins. Among its highest mountains is **Mount Ararat** (5137 m.a.s.l.), where the remains of Noah's Ark are believed to have been found.

With a marked Armenian influence, it has a continental climate, with harsh and long winters with average temperatures of −20° C and short summers, with temperatures around 20° C. Due to its high snowfalls, it is a favorite destinations for snow sports.

Aged cheeses are produced in this region, made with goat or lamb's milk. Its kebabs and dishes prepared with lamb meat are famous.

In **Erzurum**, architecture dating from the 12th and 16th centuries stand out, such as the **Çifte** and the **Yakutiye Medresesi**, located in the center of the city. **In Kars**, the archaeological ruins of the **Church of the 12 Apostles** in Ani are also of great interest.

Erzurum is famous for its **Cağ Kebab** (see page 94) and its **Kadayıf Dolması**. While in **Kars**, dishes with yogurt or tomato sauce feature prominently, such as the case of its famous **Hangel** (see page 100), a dish prepared with a flour dough and a delicious yogurt sauce seasoned with garlic.

ÇAĞ KEBAB

Serves 6-8

Ingredients
Ingredients
1 leg of lean lamb (without fat and nerves)
100g yogurt
1 tsp black pepper
1 tsp salt
1 onion

For Ganrishing
lavash bread
4 tomatoes
6-7 green peppers

You will also need:
Kebab skewers
A grill to cook the kebabs, preferably a coal one.

Step 1: Slice the leg into pieces about the width of a finger.

Step 2: Mix yogurt, black pepper, salt, and chopped onion and leave the meat in this marinade for 24 hours.

Step 3: The next day, layer the thin slices of meat, one on top of the other, onto the skewer and cook the kebab by laying it horizontally over the fire.

Step 4: Cook the tomato and green pepper on the fire and serve it with your kebab over lavaş bread.

KADAYIF DOLMASI
Stuffed kadayıf

Serves 6-8

Ingredients
For the syrup
1 cup sugar
1 cup water
few drops of lemon juice

For the kadayıf rolls
200g kadayıf (see page 38)
1/2 cup coarsely chopped walnuts
4 eggs – beaten
Enough vegetable oil to deep-fry your kadayıf

For garnishing
Powdered pistachios

For the syrup
Step 1: Bring the sugar and water to a to boil in a heavy-bottomed pot for about 10 minutes. Add the lemon juice. Set aside.

For the kadayıf rolls
Step 2: Spread the kadayıf out in strips of about 30x10cm. Chop the walnuts into small pieces with a knife and place them to one end of the strips of kadayıf threads. Roll them up into cylinders. Repeat the process until you run out of kadayıf.

Step 3: Dip each roll into the beaten egg and press them with your hands to absorb enough liquid.

Step 4: Deep-fry in hot oil until it turns crispy and golden brown. Pour into the cold syrup and leave to rest for a minimum of 20 minutes before serving.

Step 5: Sprinkle with some powdered pistachio for decoration.

COOKING
WITH
YASEMIN
KILIÇ

- Kars

I met Yasemin in my first weeks in Ankara, when I was beginning to learn Turkish, and she didn't speak a single word of English. She's quite shy and very respectful. We had funny conversations, in our broken English/Turkish, and most of the time, we understood the opposite of what we wanted to say, but we still managed to communicate. She taught me common words in Turkish, the names of everyday objects, numbers, and, most importantly, the terms used for cooking ingredients and kitchen utensils. For me, it was imperative to make her part of this book because, in my opinion, she represents the authenticity of Turkish cuisine, home cooking, a mother's food. Yasemin is a living example of the gastronomic baggage that Turkish people carry within them from the moment they are born.

❝ I was born in 1977 and am originally from Kars. I am the mother of two children. I live in Ankara. I learned how to cook from my mother. My mom is a wonderful cook and makes lovely meals."

ERIŞTE
ⲠILAVI

Serves 6-8

Ingredients
For the dough
500g flour
Salt
2 eggs
100ml water

For the Erişte
2 tbsp butter
1 ½ cups hot water
2 tbsp olive oil
1 potato
Salt to taste

For the syrup
Step 1: Put 400g of flour into a bowl. Add salt and eggs. Add the water slowly and mix well, forming an elastic dough, which does not stick to the fingers. If necessary, add a little more flour. Knead the dough until it has a firm consistency and split it into two parts. Using a rolling pin, roll out the dough to about the thickness of a lasagna sheet. Cut into 3x3cm squares and then cut each square into strips about half a centimeter wide. You can use this dough immediately or allow it to air dry and store it in an airtight container.

Preparing the Erişte Ⲣilavı
Step 2: Cut the potatoes into 1/2-inch-wide slices and fry in oil until golden brown and soft. Set aside.

Step 3: In a frying pan, melt the butter and add the Erişte pılavı. Stirring constantly, cook for three minutes or until it begins to brown.

Step 4: In. Serve with the previously cooked potatoes.

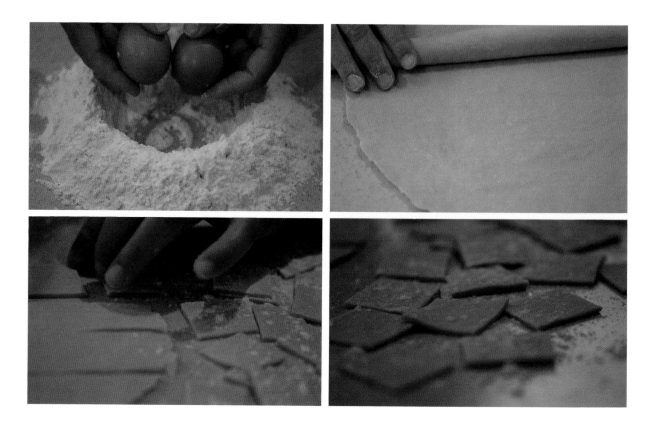

HANGEL

Serves 6-8

Ingredients
2 liters of water
1 tsp salt
1 tsp olive oil
400g + 100 g of flour
Salt
2 eggs
100ml water

For the yogurt sauce
3 garlic cloves
300g plain yogurt

For the carmelized onions
1 medium dried onion
100ml sunflower or olive oil
50g butter

For garnishing
1 tbsp butter
2 tsp pul biber
(powdered red pepper)

Step 1: Put 2 liters of water into a large pot and bring to a boil. Add salt and olive oil. Let the water cool off a bit before adding to the mixture.

Step 2: Put 400g of flour into a separate bowl. Add the salt and eggs. Slowly add the water and mix well, forming an elastic dough, which does not stick to the fingers. If necessary, add a little more flour. Knead the dough until it has a firm consistency. Divide this dough in two parts.

Step 3: Using a rolling pin, roll out the dough to more or less the height of lasagna pasta. Cut into 3x3cm squares and add to the pot with water and bring to a boil for 10 minutes.

Preparing the yogurt sauce
Step 4: Crush the garlic and mix it with yogurt.

Preparing the onions
Step 5: Julienne the onions and sauté them in a pan with sunflower oil. Keep stirring them until they turn brown, then add the butter and mix. Set aside.

Plating your hangel
Step 6: Add some of the strained yogurt to the bottom of your serving plate, add the boiled dough and cover it with the remaining yogurt on top. Finish by adding the caramelized onion.

For garnishing
Step 7: Melt the butter in a pan and add the powdered red pepper. Cook until it starts to foam. Add this sauce on the top of your hangel.

KURU FASULYE ÇORBASI
(Dried white beans soup)

Serves 6-8

Ingredients
2 tbsp butter
3 tbsp olive oil
1 medium onion – chopped
2 tbsp tomato paste
500g white beans – soaked in water for at least 12 hours before use
1 tsp powdered red pepper
1 tsp granulated sugar
Salt to taste
1½ liters of hot water
Salt to taste

Step 1: In the pot where you will cook your soup, melt the butter and oil over a medium heat. Add the chopped onion and cook until it turns translucent.

Step 2: Add the tomato paste and cook for 3 minutes. Add the beans that you have soaked for at least 12 hours and mix well. Add the powdered chili pepper, sugar, and salt. Mix and cover with the water. Cook until the beans are soft. Season with salt and serve hot.

SOUTHEASTERN ANATOLIA

This is one of my favorite regions in Turkey and perhaps the one I visited the most during my 5 years living in the country.

On the border with Syria and Iraq, part of this region is washed by the Euphrates and Tigris rivers, which are mentioned in various books of the Old and New Testaments of the Bible. The archaeological sites, the old churches, mesquites, and madrasas are mixed with a culture and architecture very different from that of the rest of the country.

Sanliurfa, Diyarbakır and **Mardin**, located on the silk trading route, have significant Assyrian and Armenian influence. It is believed that the prophet Abraham lived in the lands of Sanliurfa and that the apostle Thomas himself founded the Christian church in this city. His remains were buried in one of its old churches, today converted into Mesquites or museums.

This region is characterized by having a semi-arid continental climate, with very hot summers and cold winters. It has a rich archeology that continues to be discovered. Mosaics and buildings dating back at least 3,000 years are found here. Thanks to its strategic location on the **Silk Road,** the use of a vast variety of spices stands out in each of its impressive recipes.

Mardin, a part of historical Mesopotamia, where a strong Arab influence is evident in its arquitecture. The walls of its buildings were built in an orange mud that gives a mystical air to the city. The Arab and Armenian influence is also present in its gastronomy, a true confluence of cultures. Its mezes and main dishes mix fruits such as green plums, with meat, usually lamb. A very famous dish in this city is its **Kaburga Dolması** (see recipe on page 120), which consists of lamb ribs stuffed with rice previously prepared with dried fruits and walnuts and which is a feast for the eyes and the palate.

In **Gaziantep,** famous for its pistachios and baklava (see recipe on page 107), it is common in the summer months to see city balconies full of colorful vegetables drying in the sun. The mezes with olives, olive oil and, obviously, pistachios, stand out in this city, as well as the use of both fresh and sun-dried vegetables.

Several kebabs also stand out in this city, prepared not only with meat, but also with vegetables such as eggplants and onions or a mixture of both. Their **Beyran çorba,** a spicy soup, prepared with lamb meat and a stock that is cooked for hours over a fire, is delicious as well as nutritious. Historically it is consumed early in the morning, before starting the workday.

Gaziantep was included in 2015 in the **Creative Cities Network** for its gastronomy. Every year, renowned chefs from different parts of the world meet at various festivals to promote their gastronomic products. The city government has created a network of programs to protect and promote its heritage.

BAKLAVA

Serves 6-8

Ingredients
For the stuffing
750ml milk
75g semolina
500g ground pistachios

For the syrup
1kg sugar
450ml water
1 kg sugar
1 tbsp lemon juice

For the dough
1kg flour
1 tsp salt
3 eggs
2 cups flour starch
1 cup (clarified butter)

For the filling
Step 1: Bring the milk and semolina to a boil in a heavy-bottomed saucepan, constantly stirring until the mixture begins to boil. Set aside until cool.

For the syrup
Step 2: Mix the water with the sugar and lemon juice and bring it all to a boil for 10 minutes. Set aside.

For the dough
Step 3: Preheat the oven to 200°C.

Step 4: Put the flour onto a flat surface and mix with the salt. Then arrange it in a volcano shape and place the eggs and enough water in the center. Mix well with your hands and knead to form a flexible dough, which does not stick to the fingers. Continue kneading for about 5 minutes.

Step 5: Divide the dough into 40 equal parts. Spread a little starch on the surface and start rolling each piece with a rolling pin in circular shapes of approximately 50 cm in diameter, adding starch to stretch each dough circle.

Step 6: Grease a baking tray of approximately 50 cm in diameter with ghee and begin to place your circles of dough, adding a little ghee between one sheet of dough and another. When you have 20 sheets assembled, carefully add the semolina filling and cover it with the ground pistachio. Add more ghee and continue laying out the rest of the dough sheets, adding ghee in between.

Step 7: Finally, use a sharp knife to cut the squares approximately 2x2cm. Add the rest of the ghee and bake until golden. Remove it from the oven.

Step 8: Pour the syrup over the still-hot baklava and let it sit until cool.

ÇEVIRMELI PILAV

(upside down rice)

Serves 6-8

Ingredients
2 tbsp pistachio
2 tbsp almonds
2 tbsp raisins
500 g rice
6 eggplants
1/4 cup vegetable oil
5 racks of Lamb Chops
2 tbsp olive oil
2 tbsp ghee
1 tbsp tomato paste
1 tsp black pepper
1 tsp allspice
Salt to taste
4 cups hot water
2 tbsp pine nuts
1 tsp cinnamon

You will also need:
kitchen paper towels

Step 1: Soak the pistachio, almonds, raisins, and rice separately overnight. The following day, blanch them with boiling water. Peel the almonds and pistachios, discarding water and the skin. Set aside.

Step 2: Cover the rice with water and let it sit overnight. In the morning remove the water, wash and cover it again, this time with hot water. Let it sit until the water cools down. Set aside.

Step 3: Cut the eggplants into thin slices lengthwise and fry them in a pan with the vegetable oil until lightly browned, turning them upside-down to cook evenly on each side. Place them over kitchen paper towels to remove excess oil. Set aside.

Cooking the meat
Step 4: Sauté the meat from side to side in olive oil for about two minutes. Add ghee to the meat and sauté it for a few more minutes. Add the tomato paste, black pepper, allspice, and salt and cook for a minute. Add 4 cups of hot water, mix well, and cook until the meat softens. Take the meat out of the liquid and drain it in a colander. Keep both the meat and the stock for later.

Pre-cooking the rice
Step 5: Strain the rice through a fine strainer until all the water is removed. Add the pine nuts, raisins, and cinnamon in a pot and toast them until the aroma evaporates. Add the rice and mix well. Toast everything for two minutes. Set aside.

Assembling your dish
Step 6: In a heavy-bottomed, round pot with a lid, place the pistachios and almonds in the center. Carefully cover the sides of the pot with the eggplants, vertically, until you have a perfect lining. Add the rice, while keeping the eggplants in place. Cover everything with the leftover liquid from the meat. Cover the rice with the rest of the eggplants and place the lid on the pot. Bring this pot to a low heat until all the liquid is absorbed. Let your rice sit for 10-15 minutes before serving.

Step 7: Replace the lid with your presentation plate. Turn very carefully and firmly, grasping the pot upside down on the plate.

KARIŞIK DOLMASI
(Stuffed mixed vegetables)

Serves 6–8

Ingredients
Dried vegetables
6 small, dried eggplants
6 small, dried zucchinis

Fresh vegetables
6 small eggplants
6 small fresh zucchinis
6 medium tomatoes
6 small bell peppers

For the stuffing
1 cup rice
1 large onion
6 garlic cloves
300g lamb with fat (minced)
2 tbsp tomato paste
2 tbsp pepper paste
1 tsp allspice
1 tsp black pepper
1 tsp cumin
Salt to taste
1/4 cup water

For cooking the dolmas
4 garlic cloves
1 tbsp tomato paste
1 tbsp red pepper paste
2 tsp şumak extract or the juice one lemon
1 tbsp salt
1 1/2 cups water
2 tbsp olive oil

For the dried vegetables
Step 1: Put the dried vegetables into separate pots, cover them with water and bring them to a boil. Leave to cool. Cover with room temperature water and let them sit overnight.

For the fresh vegetables
Step 2: With the help of a dolma oyacağı (page 43) or a small knife, core the eggplants and fresh zucchinis, turning them into pockets ready to be filled. Set aside the thick part to use later. Cut the base of the tomatoes and the peppers and leave the tomato seeds and juice to mix them later with the stuffing Keep the tops part of the tomatoes and peppers to cover the dolmas during cooking. Set aside.

Preparing the stuffing
Step 3: Rinse the rice well. Mince the onion and 6 garlic cloves and mix with the minced beef, rice, tomato and pepper paste, spices, and salt. Squeeze the tomato filling you separated in the previous step, strain the juice, and add it to the mixture. Add 1/4 cup of water. Mix well.

Assembling your dolmas
Step 4: Drain the dried vegetables. Fill each of them (fresh and dried), with the meat and rice stuffing, leaving space at the top to allow the rice to expand during cooking. Cover fresh eggplants and zucchinis with the thick part that you had saved. Cover the tomatoes and bell peppers with their lids.

Cooking the dolmas
Step 5: Place the stuffed vegetables one on top of the other into a tower in a heavybottomed pot. Start with the zucchinis as they will take the longest to cook. Continue with the eggplants, the peppers, and finally the tomatoes.

Step 6: Grate the remaining four garlic cloves and mix them with a tablespoon of tomato paste, a tablespoon of pepper paste, şumak or lemon juice, and salt and dilute with one and a half cups of water. Spread over the vegetables. If you do not have a Dolma taşı, (page 43) place a plate upside-down on top of the dolmas and then cover the pot with a lid.

Step 7: Cook for an hour on low heat, making sure that the liquid does not dry out or the vegetables stick to the bottom of the pot.

KARNIYARIK
(Belly Button)

Serves 6

Ingredients
6 tomatoes
1/2 tbsp salt
1 large onion
2 tbsp olive oil
300g ground beef
1 tbsp tomato paste
1/2 tbsp pepper paste
1 tsp black pepper
1 tsp salt
1/4 cup water
Enough vegetable oil to deep-fry
6 medium eggplants
6 long green peppers
3 pear tomatoes cut into wedges
2 tbsp olive oil

Step 1: Preheat the oven to 180° C.

Step 2: Cut the tomatoes into large pieces and place them in a colander, over a bowl. Sprinkle half tablespoon of salt over the tomatoes and let them rest for 30 minutes. Squeeze them over the strainer and collect as much juice as possible. Discard the pulp.

Cooking the meat
Step 3: Dice the onion and sauté them in a pan with olive oil for two minutes or until caramelized. Add the meat and constantly stir for even cooking. Cook until all the liquids evaporate. Add the tomato paste, pepper paste, black pepper, and salt. Stir constantly to mix. Add 1/4 cup of water to help dilute the sauces. Cook for two minutes and turn off the heat. Set aside.

Cooking the eggplant
Step 5: In a heavy-bottomed pot, add enough vegetable oil to deep-fry the eggplants and bring to medium-high heat. Cut strips in the skin of the eggplants lengthwise to produce a contrast of dark and light colors and deep-fry them in the hot oil until golden brown. Remove them from the oil and place them to drain on a paper towel.

Step 6: Using the back of a spoon, open the center of the eggplant along its length and press to create a kind of pocket, paying attention not to break them. Fill with the meat and place onto a deep and spacious baking tray. Spoon the tomato juice, previously prepared in step 1 over the eggplants. Bake them in the oven for 45 minutes.

For garnishing
Step 7: In a heavy-bottomed pan, heat the oil and sauté the green chiles and tomato wedges in it until brown. Place on top of the eggplants to decorate and cook everything in the oven for an additional 5 minutes. Serve hot.

YUVARLAMA

(Rice dumplings stew with meat and yogurt)

Serves 8

Ingredients

To prepare the night before
1 1/2 cups rice
1/2 cup chickpeas

500g lamb with bones
6 cups water
Salt to taste

For the dumplings
250g lean minced lamb
1 tsp salt
1 tsp black pepper
Olive oil as needed

For the yogurt sauce
3 cups strained yogurt
1 egg
2 tbsp olive oil

For garnishing
1 tbsp butter
1 tbsp olive oil
1 tbsp dried mint
250g lean minced lamb
1 tsp black pepper
Salt to taste

The night before
Step 1: Wash the rice and soak it overnight.

Step 2: Cover the chickpeas with water and let them soak overnight.

Cooking the meat
Step 3: Cover the meat with 6 cups of water and bring it to a boil with the overnight soaked chickpeas the next day. Add salt to taste. Skim off the foam that forms on the surface and cook for at least two hours.

Meanwhile
Step 4: Let the rice drain until all the water is removed and mix with the ground beef, salt and pepper and pass it through the meat grinder several times to compact the ingredients. Knead for about 5 minutes until you get a pliable dough.

Step 5: Lightly brush your hands with olive oil and assemble the dumplings by rubbing a little of the dough in a circular motion between your hands until they form balls about the size of a chickpea. Repeat until all the dough is finished.

Step 6: Add the dumplings to the soup and cook for 15 minutes.

For the yogurt sauce
Step 7: In a small pot, add the yogurt, the egg, and two tablespoons of olive oil and cook on low heat, constantly stirring in the same direction, adding a little of the meat broth while stirring. When the yogurt begins to expand, add it to the pot of stew, and remove the pot from heat.

For garnishing the Yuvarlama
Step 8: Melt a tablespoon of butter with a tablespoon of olive oil. Sprinkle the dry mint into a ladle and pour the melted butter over it. Drizzle this mixture over the yuvarlama and serve.

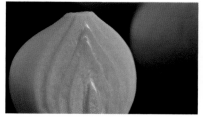  

ŞOĞAN KEBAB
(Onion Kebab)

Serves 5-6

Ingredients
18 medium onions
500g chopped fatty meat
2 teaspoon salt

For the pomegranate sauce
2 tbsp pomegranate molasses
1/2 cup water
1 tsp salt

You also will need
A zırh
Kebab skewers
A grill and charcoal

Step 1: Prepare the charcoal on your grill to be ready when you finish assembling the skewers (or preheat your gas grill).

Step 2: Remove the outer skin of the onions and delicately cut the two ends. Cut each onion in half lengthwise. Set aside.

Step 3: Mix the meat with the salt and leave aside for the next step.

Preparing your kebab skewers
Step 4: Moisten your hands and make meatballs approximately the same size of the onions (small lemons). Alternate meatballs and onions on the skewers, taking care not to hurt your fingers.

Step 5: Cook on your barbecue over a moderate heat, constantly turning the skewers to cook evenly and avoid burninng the onions. Remove the meat and onions from the skewers and discard the outer layer of the onions.

Preparing the pomegranate sauce
Step 6: In a pan, dilute the molasses into 1/2 cup of water and add a teaspoon of salt.

Preparing your kebabs
Step 7: Add your meat and onion to the pan with the pomegranate sauce and stir. Cook over low heat for 10 minutes. Serve your kebab with bread.

In Turkey, when preparing meat for kebabs, a Zırh (page 43), a special meat-chopping knife, is used. If you don't have one, try grinding the meat in the thickest setting of your meat-grinder, or ask your butcher for a coarse grind.

İROK

Makes 14

Ingredients
1 medium potato
enough water to boil the potato
A pinch of salt

For the dough
2 cups fine bulgur
2 cups hot water
1/2 cup flour
1 egg
1 tsp red pepper paste
1 tsp powdered red chili pepper
Salt to taste

For the stuffing
2 tbsp olive oil
2 medium onions – diced
150g minced meat
Salt to taste
1 tsp each of black pepper, powdered red chili pepper

Step 1: Boil the potato in a pot with water and a little salt until it softens. Mash it and keep for later.

For the dough
Step 2: Soak the bulgur in the hot water and let it sit for 10 minutes or until all the water is absorbed.

Preparing the stuffing
Step 3: In a heavy-bottomed pan, heat the oil over medium heat. Sauté the onions until they are translucent. Incorporate the meat and sauté for two minutes. Then sprinkle the salt and spices and cook for two more minutes. Remove from heat and set aside.

Preparing the dough
Step 3: Place the bulgur in a bowl, add the flour and mix well. Add the egg, mashed potato, pepper paste, red pepper powder, and salt. Knead well.

Step 4: Lightly moisten your hands and form balls about the size of a walnut. Make a pocket-shaped hole in each ball with your fingers and add a little meat to it. Close it and form sealed balls.

Step 5: Fry with enough hot oil until golden brown, and then place them on a paper towel to let the excess oil drain off. Serve hot.

Mardin city center

KABURGA DOLMASI

(stuffed ribs)

Kaburga Dolması is a celebration of food and is my favorite recipe from this city. It offers the perfect excuse to sit together at the table and enjoy the aromas and flavors of this first-class dish originally from Mardin, a city steeped in history and with an Arab influence that stands out in every part of every dish that is produced here.

To prepare this dish, consult with your butcher to choose the best piece of meat, which obviously must be as fresh and lean as possible. The inner part, prepared to be stuffed with rice, should be cut to perfection, with no gaps that could cause the filling to come out. The cooks at Mardin recommend choosing a male lamb to ensure that the meat is not too fatty.

Serves 6-8

Ingredients
1/2 cup almonds
3 cups rice
2 tbsp currants
A whole rack of lamb
(approximately 3 kg)**
3 tablespoons of butter

For the rice stuffing
1 tbsp butter
2 tbsp olive oil
2 medium onions - chopped
2 garlic cloves - chopped
1/4 cup pine nuts
1 tsp salt
1 tbsp allspice
1 tbsp powdered cumin
1 tbsp coriander seeds - pounded
2 tsp powdered cinnamon
2 tsp powdered black pepper
1/2 tbsp tomato paste
1/2 tbsp red pepper paste
7 cups water
1 handful dill - chopped
1 handful parsley - chopped

For the sauce
2 tbsp olive oil
1 tbsp tomato paste
A pinch of salt
1 tsp honey
1 tsp pomegranate molasses
1 1/2 glasses water

To assemble your kaburga
1 tbsp olive oil
Salt and black pepper to taste

You will also need
Kitchen string
A deep wire-rack roasting pan
Aluminium paper
A cooking brush

Before you start
Step 1: Preheat the oven to 175°C.

Step 2: Soak the almonds in hot water and let them rest until cool. Drain and remove the skin and set aside.

Step 3: Soak the rice in hot water and let it rest for 15 minutes. Soak the currants for 15 minutes. After 15 minutes, drain and set aside.

Preparing the stuffing
Step 4: In a large saucepan, melt the butter with one tablespoon of olive oil and add the chopped onions. Cook until they turn translucent. Add the garlic and cook for a few seconds. Add the drained and skinless almonds, pine nuts, currants, rice, salt, and spices. Sauté everything for two minutes. Add the tomato and pepper paste and mix well. Let it cook for two more minutes before covering everything with 7 cups of water. Let the rice cook until all the water evaporates, then add the chopped dill and parsley. Mix well and remove half of the rice to use it in the stuffing. Cook the other half of the rice until it is al dente and set aside to serve when plating the kaburga.

Preparing the sauce
Step 5: Heat your olive oil in a pan and add the tomato paste. Cook for two to three minutes, stirring constantly. Add salt, honey, and molasses and dilute with water. Cook for two minutes and remove from heat. Set aside.

Assembling your kaburga
Step 6: Add a little olive oil to the inside of the rack of lamb and sprinkle it with a bit of salt and pepper. Fill it with half of the precooked rice and sew up the opening with kitchen string without leaving any gaps. Sprinkle the ribs with salt and black pepper.

Step 7: Put a liter of water in a deep, wire-rack roasting tin. Place the stuffed rib on the wire rack, making sure it's not touching the water. Cover the tray with aluminum foil and bake at 175 °C for three hours. After this time, raise the temperature of your oven to 200°C and remove the aluminum foil. Use a cooking brush to spread the sauce over your rib and let it cook 15-20 minutes more or until golden brown. Remove from the oven and place on a serving tray with the rest of the rice.

** Preparing the Kaburga Dolması
Note: If your butcher has not prepared the meat and you need to prepare it yourself, take a very sharp and pointed knife and open a pocket in the ribs cutting the meat parallel to the bones, taking care not to make any unnecessary holes. Expand this open pocket along the entire rib using your fist. You must have enough space between the rib bones and the meat for the stuffing.

REYHAN ŞERBETI
(Purple Basil Cold Drink)

Serves 6–8

Ingredients
1 bunch of purple basil
2 liters hot water
1 cup sugar
juice of one lemon
1 cinnamon stick
1/4 tsp cloves
2 liters hot water

Step 1: Wash the purple basil leaves well. Dry them and put them in a large jar.

Step 2: Put the water in a heavy-bottomed pot and dissolve the sugar in it. Place the pot on the stove over a medium heat and add the cinnamon and cloves. Leave it over the heat until it starts to boil. Remove from heat.

Step 3: Pour this still hot mixture over the basil leaves and let them rest until cool. Add the lemon juice and cover the pitcher with a clean cloth. Let it sit overnight. After this time, strain your sherbet and chill it in the fridge or serve immediately with ice.

KİLİŞ KEBAB
(Twice cooked eggplant kebab)

The kiliş kebab is cooked twice. A first light cooking on skewers and over charcoal, called tavlanma, which adds a flavor that is only achieved with charcoal cooking. The second cooking is on the stove, prepared with a sauce that enhances the taste of this delicious dish.

Serves 6–8

Ingredients
For the first cooking
1 1/2 kg eggplants
500g lamb – fatty
2 tsp salt
1 tsp allspice
1 tsp ground black pepper

For second cooking
1 tbsp tomato paste
1 tbsp red pepper paste
1/4 cup water
2 tsp salt
juice of one lemon
1/2 tsp allspice
1/2 tsp black pepper
2 tbsp butter
1 tbsp olive oil
2 medium onions – cut into wedges
3 medium tomatoes – diced
2 green chili peppers – sliced

You also will need:
A zırh (special knife to chop the meat of the kebabs –see page 43)

For the first cooking
Step 1: Peel the eggplants and cut them in half lengthwise. Then cut each part into quarters. Set aside.

Step 2: Chop the meat with the zırh (page 43) a sharp knife and try not to over-grind it. Mix with salt, allspice, and ground black pepper. Knead to mix.

Step 3: Assemble skewers by alternating pieces of eggplant and meatballs, moistening your hands to form meatballs roughly the size of walnuts. Cook lightly over the charcoal, turning constantly to prevent the meat from drying out and the eggplants from burning. Remove from skewers and set aside for the next step.

For the second cooking

Preparing the sauce
Step 4: Dilute the tomato and red pepper pastes with 1/4 cup of hot water. Add salt, lemon, and spices. Mix well.

Cooking the kiliş kebab
Step 5: In a deep pot, melt the butter over medium heat together with the oil. Add the onions and sauté them until they turn translucent. Add the tomatoes and green pepper and cook for two minutes. Add the precooked meat and the slightly pre-cooked eggplants and mix gently, paying attention not to break the meatballs. Pour the pre-cooked sauce over the meat and mix very carefully. Cover everything with hot water and cook over low heat for 45 minutes.

AĞZI ACIK
(Open Mouth)

Makes 18

Ingredients
For the dough
250g flour
1/4 cup vegetable oil
1/3 cup plain yogurt
5g yeast
1 tsp salt
¼ cup water

For the stuffing

125g ground beef
¼ onion
1 tbsp flour
½ egg
1 tsp powdered red pepper
1 tsp powdered cinnamon
1 tsp powdered cloves
1 tsp ground black pepper
1 tsp powdered cumin
1 tsp crushed coriander seeds
1 tsp salt
Enough vegetable oil for deep-frying your patties

You will also need:
Paper towels

Step 1: Place the flour in a bowl and add the oil, yogurt, yeast, salt, and 1/2 cup of water. Mix to form an elastic dough that does not stick to your fingers. If necessary, add a little more flour or water. Knead well for a few minutes until you get a smooth dough. Roll out into circles 10 cm in diameter. Cover them with a clean cloth and set them aside for the next step.

Preparing the stuffing
Step 2: In a bowl, mix the beef with the rest of the ingredients and knead well with your hands to ensure that all the elements are well combined.

Assembling your dish
Step 3: Moisten the center of each dough circle a little with your hands and place a small portion of the meat mixture, pressing down with your fingers to stick it to the dough.

Step 4: Hem the edge of the patty to secure the dough and fry in hot oil, starting with the beef part up and then turning them around to cook evenly. Your patty will be ready when they turn a light golden-brown color. Remove them from the heat and drain the excess oil over a paper towel.

Variety of chilies drying in the sun in summer on the balconies of İzmir

ÆGEAN REGION

Characterized by a beautiful landscape, with countless beaches with pristine waters lapping its coasts and cliffs, the Aegean region is a destination that is generally associated with water sports, good food and fun. Its green mountains, perpendicular to its coasts, protect the extensive valleys, allowing the circulation of the marine air towards the interior of the region, creating a mild climate, ideal for farming. Its summers are hot and dry, and winters are usually mild.

Like elsewhere in Turkey, the Aegean region is a perfect destination for archeology lovers, as it has a diversity of ruins dating back hundreds of years. In this region are the famous ruins of Ephesus, in İzmir, an ancient city with many legends about how it was founded. One of them tells that the city was built by the Amazons, a tribe of female warriors at the end of the Bronze Age in honor of the mother goddess. The truth is that this ancient city was the most important trading center for the Mediterranean throughout centuries. The ruins were recognized in 2015 by UNESCO as a World Heritage site, and are impressively well-preserved. It is a destination visited by millions of tourists every year.

İzmir is also host to the ruins of the House of the Virgin Mary, which is said to have been her last resting place after having escaped from Jerusalem after the death of Jesus.

İn agriculture, about half of the olives produced in the country are grown in the Aegean region. Naturally therefore, their dishes and mezes are usually accompanied by delicious olives and a variety of high-quality olive oils. Other products grown in this region are pomegranate, sugar and tobacco, among others. The marble industry is also an important means of production.

ꝹÜGÜLÜ HAŞHAŞ

(Hooked poppy)

Serves 6–8

Ingredients
1/2 cup fine bulgur
1/2 cup crushed walnuts
1 cup poppy seeds
1 cup sugar
3 1/2 cups milk
2 tbsp margarine
1 tsp grated orange zest

For garnishing
1/2 cup crushed walnuts
or 6 orange slices

In a hot pan, toast the bulgur, crushed walnuts, poppy seeds, and sugar. Add the milk little by little and mix well. Add margarine and orange zest and mix it until the margarine melts. Stir it until it has the consistency of custard. Pour it into your molds and allow it to set in the fridge. Serve it cold, garnished with crushed walnuts or with an orange slice.

ÇIĞ DOLMA

(Raw Stuffing)

Serves 2

Ingredients
1 onion
2+1 tbsp olive oil
1/2 cup coarse bulgur
1 tomato
1 bunch parsley – finely chopped
1 bunch dill – finely chopped
1 bunch scallions – finely chopped
1 bunch mint – finely chopped
Salt to taste
1 tsp black pepper
1 tsp pul biber (powdered red chili pepper)
Juice of one lemon

Step 1: Dice the onion and fry it in 2 tablespoons of olive oil until it turns translucent. Add the bulgur and mix. Cover it with hot water and let it boil.

Step 2: Grate the tomato with a cheese grater and add it to the bulgur. The bulgur should be cooked and juicy. Mix and remove it from heat.

Step 3: Add the finely chopped vegetables and season it with salt, red pepper, and crushed black pepper. Add the lemon juice and the rest of the olive oil and mix well to combine.

ZEYTINYAĞLI TAZE FASULYE

(Green beans with olive oil)

Serves 6–8

Ingredients
500g green beans
½ liter hot water
2 medium onions
4 garlic cloves
3 large tomatoes
¼ cup olive oil
1 tbsp sugar
1 tsp salt
1/2 liter hot water

Step 1: Slice the green beans lengthwise, cutting them in half. Cut the onions into wide julienne strips. Cut the garlic into large chunks. Peel the tomatoes and cut them into wide julienne strips.

Step 2: Heat the olive oil in a heavy-bottomed pot and add all the vegetables, sugar and salt. Pour over 1/2 liter of hot water.

Step 3: Cover the pot with kitchen paper and simmer for 30 minutes or until the green beans are cooked. Remove from heat and leave to cool. This dish is served cold.

BLACK SEA REGION

Occupying 18% of the entire Turkish territory, the Black Sea region is characterized by its abrupt, rocky coasts and green mountains. It has a temperate oceanic climate, with warm summers and cold winters. The constant rains allow for unequalled flora and fauna and have given way to the formation of beautiful and impressive waterfalls, as well as fertile rivers and countless lakes.

The sharp contrast of the sea with the intense green of the mountains stands out. While its coasts are rich in many varieties of fish, its mild and humid climate favors agriculture; its main crops being hazelnuts, black tea, corn, rice, beans, and potatoes.

The region's population is mainly concentrated in the coastal areas.

Due to the presence of abundant seafood in the area, its delicious mezes are usually prepared with these ingredients. This is the case of **Hamsi Tava** (see recipe on page 61), a delicious dish prepared with boneless anchovies, which are breaded and fried in the shape of the pan. It is one of the most consumed seafood mezes in the entire country. Kuymak, a dish of melted cheese, is also very common in this region.

What's more, embedded in the cliffs of the mountains of the Altındere National Park in Trabzon in the Black Sea region, are the ruins of **Sumela**, a Greek Orthodox monastery. According to legend, the monastery was built in 386 AC by two priests who found an image of the Virgin Mary (All Holy in Greek) in a cave in these mountains.

Trabzon is a coastal city with strong commercial and tourism links to Saudi Arabia, which are reflected in the daily life of this city. During the summer and autumn months, it is a real spectacle to visit this city, since its sidewalks are covered with hazelnuts that have been left to dry in the sun. Impressive tea crops can also be seen in its hills.

The city of **Bolu**, on the other hand, famous throughout the country for giving birth to many chefs and gastronomy professionals who today work in restaurants and hotels around the country, is also in this region. It is a city that also has impressive mountains, covered with pine trees and beautiful lakes that are a popular local tourist destination, both in summer for its fresh climate, and in winter when several snow sports are offered.

UN HELVASI

(Flour halvah)

Serves 6-8

Ingredients
2 cups flour
1 cup icing sugar – sifted
200g + 1 tsp butter
1/2 cup ground pistachios

Step 1: Heat a heavy-bottomed pot over a medium heat. Add the flour and toast it for 15 minutes without adding any fat, constantly stirring with a wooden spoon to prevent the flour from burning. Remove from the heat. Then pass the roasted flour through a sieve, add the sifted icing sugar, mix well.

Step 2: Melt the butter and add it while still hot to the flour. Mix the ingredients well.

Step 3: Grease a 24 cm diameter mold with butter and transfer your dough to it. Press down with the a wooden spoon or the bottom of a cup to make a compact, even cake. Let it set for two hours in the fridge before unmolding.

Step 4: Cut as desired and garnish with a little crushed pistachio.

ŞÜTLAÇ
(Rice pudding)

Serves 6–8

Ingredients
1 cup rice
2 cups water
5 1/2 cups milk
3 tbsp büğday nişastasi
(wheat starch)
1 cup sugar
1 tsp vanilla

For garnishing
1/2 cup ground pistachios
1/2 cup ground walnuts

Step 1: Preheat the oven to 180°C.

Step 2: In a heavy-bottomed pot, cook the rice with water over medium heat until soft. Add the milk, wheat starch, sugar, and vanilla and mix to integrate all the ingredients. Cook for about 10 minutes, constantly stirring so that the mixture does not stick to the pot.

Step 3: Transfer the mixture to ramekins and place them on a baking tray in a bain-marie. Bake until golden brown.

Step 4: Let your Sütlaç cool to room temperature and garnish with pistachio and crushed walnuts. Refrigerate and serve it cold.

Galata Tower in İstanbul

Photo by Fatmanur

Marmara Region

The **Marmara region** is the point at which the European and Asian continents join. The crossroads for hundreds of tribes and civilizations passing through for thousands of years. It is, therefore, a region of unprecedented cultural diversity. Its landscapes and buildings live and breathe the history of the empires that have imbued its cities with such cultural wealth.

Its most iconic city, İstanbul (15,462,452 population – December 2020), is the largest city in Turkey and the most populous in the entire European continent. It was, for hundreds of years, home to the most important empires in the history of mankind.

Walking through the center of Istanbul is comparable to taking a trip back in time. Walk alongside the walls of **Old Constantinople,** or visit the impressive **Hagia Sophia** or the **Blue Mosque.** Stroll through the gardens of **Topkapı,** where **Turkish Cuisine** as we know today first came into being or visit the **Dolmabache.** One can easily imagine Byzantines, Romans, Greeks, and Ottomans, walking through each part of this magnificent city. Few countries in the world have as much shared and millennial history as that found in this vivid city, which is divided not only between Europe and Asia, but also between the beauty of its historic buildings juxtaposed with the imposing modernity of newer ones.

Strolling through the **Grand Bazaar** imbues any visitor with that living mix of culture and history. The scents of a variety of spices pervade the air along with the bright colors of Turkish lamps as well as the many languages, because in the Grand Bazaar there are no unknown languages for vendors who try, always with a smile, to attract the attention of visitors to buy their colorful products. There are rugs and nuts. There is much talk, bargaining, and many cups of tea. And even more enticing than this, are the good humor and kindness of the Turkish merchants. After leaving this miniature city, you are ready to enter the metropolis.

Istanbul is also home to the most modern restaurants whose chefs, many of whom are culinary artists, have fun, day and night, presenting their delicious novelties. This city also hosts important gastronomic conferences every year where renowned chefs from all over the world come together to meet and share with professional chefs and lovers of gastronomy.

For all the above, it is hardly surprising that İstanbul is the main point of call for those wishing to discover the regional gastronomies. In its streets you can find specialties and culinary offerings from each city of the country.

Also in this region, in the city of **Çanakkale,** lie the ruins of the legendary Troy, an archaeological site registered by UNESCO in 1998 as **World Heritage** site, and of which Homer wrote in his famous literary works, The Iliad and The Odyssey, in which he describes the famous Trojan War. This event has served as inspiration for countless movies and documentaries.

At the entrance to the archaeological site stands a representation of the famous **Trojan horse,** while in the center of the city of Çannakale you can visit the version of the horse that was used in the film produced for Hollywood.

But today Çannakale is much more than Troy; it is a small city full of life and young people, mostly university students, who fill the days and nights with music and good vibes in every corner of the city.

İn numbers...
The **Marmara region** produces 73% of the sunflowers and 30% of the country's corn. Rice, wheat, sugar, olives, grapes, and most of the citrus fruits of the country are also produced in this region. In the spring months, usually between April and May, the city of İstanbul celebrates the Tulip Festival. During this celebration, the gardens of the city are dressed in millions of these flowers, of all sizes and colors.

FIRINLANMIŞ PEYNIR TATLISI

(Baked cheese dessert)

Serves 8

Ingredients
300g unsalted fresh cheese
150g butter
1 egg yolk
400g granulated sugar
250g flour
75g semolina

Step 1: Preheat the oven to 180°C.

Step 2: In a bowl, mash the cheese with a fork. Add the butter and the egg yolk and mix well to integrate the ingredients. Transfer to a heavy-bottomed saucepan and cook over medium heat until the cheese is melted. Add sugar, flour, and semolina and mix well. Remove from the heat.

Step 3: Transfer the mixture to a baking sheet and press it down with a wooden spoon. Bake in your preheated oven until the cake is golden brown. Remove from the oven and let it rest for 5 minutes before cutting. Keep it in the refrigerator until serving.

İSTANBUL

İstanbul is the gateway between Europe and the Middle East. It is where everything converges. A city steeped in the history of ancient civilizations that came together here and marked its destiny. A place where the modern meets the traditional. It shares a border with Greece and Bulgaria in Europe, but the geographical line that unites them is not only physical. History in this part of the world has allowed for the development of a regional culture with much in common. Gastronomy reflects this.

With the conquest of Constantinople by the Ottomans, Turkish cuisine underwent its most radical transformation ever. It was in the kitchen of Top Kapi, the administrative center of the Ottoman Empire, where the first touches were made to what is known today as Ottoman cuisine.

In Topkapi, particular importance was given to preparing the dishes, mastering existing techniques, and importing new ingredients to be added to the traditional ones.

With its history, art, and bridges over the Bosphorus, Istanbul is the city that most encapsulates the true essence of Turkey.

HÜNKAR BEĞENDI

(The favorite of the sultan)

Serves 4

Ingredients
For the meat
3 tbsp vegetable oil
1 onion – chopped
2 garlic cloves– chopped
1 tomato – finely diced
1 tbsp tomato paste
200g beef cut into 2x2cm cubes
1 cup hot water
Salt and pepper to taste

For the Beğendi (Eggplant béchamel)
3 eggplants
1 tbsp butter
1 tbsp of flour
1 liter of milk at room temperature
1 cup grated stringy cheese
1 tsp salt

For the garnish
1 tbsp olive oil
3 long green chilies
3 cocktail tomatoes

You will also need
Plastic film

For the meat
Step1: In a heavy–bottomed skillet, sauté the chopped onion in the oil until it turns translucent. Add the garlic and cook for 1 minute. Add the diced tomato and cook until it begins to lose its juice. Put in the meat and seal it well. Let cook for 5 minutes, stirring it from time to time to avoid burning. Add the tomato paste and cook for two more minutes. Cover with hot water and cook until the meat is tender. Salt and pepper to taste, mix and remove from heat. Set aside.

For the Beğendi (Eggplant bechamel)
Step 2: Prick the unpeeled eggplants with the tip of a sharp knife and grill them over charcoal or whatever way you like.

Step 3: Leave your eggplants to rest covered with plastic film until cool. Peel them and discard the skin. Cut into small cubes.

Step 4: In a pan, melt the butter over a medium heat and add the flour. Let it toast until lightly browned. Add the roasted eggplants, mix well and mash them with a fork. Remove the pan from the heat and add room temperature milk. Mix well to combine all the ingredients and return the hot pot to the heat. Add the cheese and salt. Mix and remove from heat. Set aside.

For the garnish
Step 5: Heat the oil in a skillet over medium–high heat, add the chilies and tomatoes, and grill until lightly browned. Set aside.

Plating your Hünkar Beğendi
Step 6: Serve your Hünkar Beğendi by spreading the eggplant béchamel on a deep plate. Place the meat over the bed of eggplant and garnish with roasted chilies and tomatoes.

Alicia's tip: By grilling the eggplants on charcoal, you add a more intense and delicious taste.

ŞULTANAHMET KÖFTESI
(Sultan Ahmed meatballs)

Serves 6–8

Ingredients
600g ground beef
1 onion finely chopped
1 garlic clove finely chopped
2 tsp salt
1 tsp black pepper
1 tsp cumin
1 1/4 cup breadcrumbs
1 tsp baking soda
Enough vegetable oil for deep-frying

For the sauce
*3 tbsp powdered
red chili*
2 tbsp grape vinegar
1 tsp olive oil
1 tsp salt

For garnishing
Some fresh vegetables of your choice
Pita bread

You will also need:
Plastic film

Preparing the meat
Step 1: In a bowl, mix the meat with the onion, garlic, salt, and spices. Knead with your hands to combine the ingredients. Add the breadcrumbs and baking soda and continue kneading until all the ingredients are well incorporated. Roll the meat and wrap it in plastic film. Refrigerate overnight.

Frying the Sultanahmet köftesı
Step 2: The next day, remove the meat from the fridge and shape it into approximately 4x8cm cylinders. Deep-fry in vegetable oil until they turn brown.

Remove from the oil and let them rest on paper towels to remove excess fat.

Preparing the sauce
Step 3: On a salad bowl, put all the ingredients and mix well with a whisk. Serve this sauce with the köfte with some vegetables over a pita bread.

MEDITERRANEAN REGION

The **Turkish Mediterranean region** ranges from the touristy, pristine beaches of the **Antalya** coast with many archaeological sites, to the historic city of Hatay, on the Syrian border. It is a region of plains, with very hot summers and mild winters.

It is an extremely fertile region and acts as orchard to the entire country. Their crops vary between citrus, grapes, cereals, and rice. Due to its climate, ideal for agriculture, 80% of all citrus fruits produced in Turkey are grown in this region. In recent years this region has launched the cultivation of products that are typically exclusive to more tropical climates, such as banana, mango, papaya, avocado, sweet potato and, more recently, cassava.

Adana, located in the southeastern Mediterranean of Turkey, was the first industrialized city in the country and one of the most productive in the region. It is famous for its production of textiles and cement. Watermelon, grapefruit, peanuts, corn, wheat, honey, cotton, sunflowers, among other agricultural products, are also grown on its land. It is famous throughout the country for its delicious **Adana Kebab** (see recipe on page 146), which has been registered by the Adana Chamber of Commerce since 2005, in order to preserve the quality of this dish. For this, they carry out courses supervised and certified by the Chamber of Commerce to train cooks throughout the city.

The historic Hatay, the southernmost city of the country, on the border with Syria, is one of the Turkish cities recognized by UNESCO in the **Creative Cities Network** thanks to its gastronomy. Located on the way of the ancient **Silk Road,** various cultures have come together in its lands over the years, creating a unique and varied gastronomy. The use of various spices stands out, which, together with an excellent olive oil, enhances its mainly vegetarian dishes. Its most famous dessert, the **künefe** (see recipe on page 161) is prepared all over the country. The municipality of Hatay, under certain policies and strategies, guarantees both the protection and promotion of the gastronomic culture and history of this interesting city.

COOKING
WITH
CHEF ILHAN
OZKAN

-Adana

Ilhan is a chef specializing in Adana cuisine. I met him when I was studying professional cooking at the Turkish Culinary Academy, and we were learning how to prepare Adana Kebab in the Turkish Cuisine module. Our practices in the restaurant's kitchen where Ilhan works in Ankara were very productive. We soon learned the techniques for several dishes typical of Adana's cuisine, largely thanks to his support, patience, and gifted teaching. When I began to visualize this book and what I wanted to convey with it, it was clear that Ilhan had to be part of it, not only because of his knowledge of his hometown kitchen but also because of his kindness and charisma, both characteristics that define the Turkish people.

Born in 1978, Ilhan started working as a cook at the age of 13. Later he worked as a chef for the Turkish diplomatic representation in countries such as Taiwan and Hong Kong. Upon his return to Ankara, Ilhan began working as an **Executive Chef** for renowned **Kebab** restaurants.

'I learned how to prepare Adana kebabs when I was very young, working and learning on the job'.

For Ilhan, the use of a **Zırh** when preparing meat for kebabs is essential as it allows for a more tender and juicier meat, in addition to improving the overall texture of the kebab.

ΛDANA KEBAB

Classic Adana Kebab
Serves 4
Ingredients
500g lamb
150g lard
2 tsp salt

Spicy Adana Kebab
Serves 4
Ingredients
500g lamb
150g lard
3 capri Peppers
2 tbsp red chili powder
1 tsp salt

Beyti Adana Kebab –
Serves 4

Ingredients
500g lamb
150g lard
2 Capri Peppers
1 bunch parsley
2 garlic cloves
2 tsp red chilli peppers
2 tsp salt

For the classic Adana Kebab
Remove the nerves from the meat with a sharp knife and then chop it into small pieces. Chop the lard into small chunks as well. Chop meat and fat with the zırh until you get ground meat. Add salt. Knead until the ingredients are well combined.

For the spicy Adana Kebab
Prepare the meat as explained above. Chop the Capri pepper with the zırh and mix it with the lamb. Add the ground red chili and salt. Knead to integrate the ingredients.

For the Beyti Adana Kebab
Step 3: Prepare the meat as explained for classic kebab. Chop the Capri pepper, parsley, and garlic cloves with the zırh and mix with the meat. Add the ground red chili and salt. Knead to integrate the ingredients.

Cooking the kebabs
Place the meats on the skewers and cook on the grill, turning the skewers from time to time to avoid burning the meat. Serve with the Adana Onion Salad (see page 148) and lavaş bread (page 90).

ADANA ONION SALAD

Serves 6–8

Ingredients
3 medium red onions
2 tbsp şumak
1 bunch parsley
juice of 1/2 lemon
3 tbsp olive oil
*1 tsp powdered red
chili pepper*
1 tsp salt

Step 1: Cut the onion into thin julienne and mix it with the şumak. Chop the parsley and add to the onion. Add the lemon juice, olive oil, and powdered chili pepper, and mix well. Add salt just before serving to prevent your salad from losing too much liquid.

Cooking with Chef Gursel Cıloğulları

-Adana

Gürsel Hanım is one of the owners and is in charge of logistics at the Turkish Culinary Academy. She is the one who makes everything work as it should. But her passion is cooking, beyond any doubt. She is a chef by profession, and at TCA, she coordinates classes with the staff and guest chefs. She has cooked live for the Tastes & Spices program broadcast on Natura TV for the entire African continent. She is a great connoisseur and a lover of Turkish cuisine. She has specialized in Turkish Mediterranean cuisine, as Adana is her hometown, but she can prepare any of the thousands of Turkish cuisine recipes. Gürsel shared invaluable culinary advice with me from the moment we met; from where to find the best varieties of vegetables and how to negotiate in Turkish markets, to how to present the dishes. She also taught me how to work the ingredients directly with my hands, to feel their texture and quality. She shared her spices and countless tips. When I asked her if she wanted to be part of my project, without hesitation, she answered "YES, I would be very happy to share my secrets in your book."

❝ I was born in 1960 in Adana. Since 2006, I have been teaching traditional Turkish cuisine as an instructor chef at the Turkish Culinary Academy. I am originally from Gaziantep and have extensive knowledge of the cuisine of south and southeast Turkey. I met with Alicia at our school and we developed a good friendship. I am really happy to share my culinary secrets in this book!"

EL TURŞUSU

(Hand picklets)

Serves 6-8

Ingredients
2 eggplants
2 zucchinis
20 long green peppers
(asorted hot and sweet)
2 garlic cloves
1 tbsp dried mint
1 tbsp şumak
Salt to taste
1 tbsp dried mint

Step 1: Finely chop the eggplants, peppers, and zucchinis and bring them to a boil over medium heat until they soften. Then remove from the heat and allow to cool.

Step 2: Crush the garlic cloves and mix together with the şumak and salt. Add the dried mint and mix. Season and serve it at room temperature.

YÖRESEL KISIR

(Regional kisir)

Serves 6-8

Ingredients
250g fine bulgur
1 cup hot water
1 tomato
5 garlic cloves
1 medium onion
2 red capia peppers
1 cucumber
A small bunch of parsley
A small bunch of mint
A small bunch of scallion
1 tbsp tomato paste
1 tbsp red pepper paste
1 tsp cumin
1 tsp powdered red pepper
1 tsp black pepper
Pomegranate syrup to taste
2 tbsp olive oil
Salt to taste

Step 1: In a bowl, cover the bulgur with the hot water, and let it sit covered with a damp cloth until all the water has been absorbed.

Step 2: Chop the tomato, garlic, onion, capia peppers, cucumber and all the herbs separately. Set aside.

Step 3: Mix the bulgur with tomato paste, pepper paste, onion, garlic, and spices. Knead with your hands until smooth.

Step 4: Add the rest of the ingredients and mix well with your hands. Check the taste and, if necessary, add a little more of the pomegranate syrup, olive oil, and salt.

In Turkish cuisine the use of hands in the preparation of dishes is of vital importance. It is a way of 'feeling' the food and each of its ingredients

Serves 6-8

Ingredients
50g rice
50g green lentils
50g farro
2 liters water
50g green beans
2 eggplants
2 bunches purslane
2 zucchinis
1 medium onion
2 tbsp olive oil
3-4 cloves garlic –chopped
1 tbsp tomato
paste
1/2 tbsp red pepper
powder

For garnishing
2 tbsp butter
1 tbsp dried mint
1 tbsp red pepper
powder
Salt to taste

CAKILDAKLI ÇORBA

(Pebble soup)

Step 1: Cook together the rice, lentils and farro in a heavy-bottomed pot with 2 liters of water for 10 minutes.

Step 2: Chop the green beans, eggplants, purslane, and zucchini and add them to the pot. Cook until soft.

Step 3: Finely chop the onion and sauté in a pan with olive oil until translucent. Add the chopped garlic cloves and cook for one minute. Mix the tomato paste and powdered red pepper. Add this mixture to the pot with the vegetables.

For Garnishing
Step 4: In a small skillet, melt the butter and pour over the dried mint and red pepper powder. Mix well and pour it over the soup. Add salt to taste. Serve hot.

FELLAH KÖFTESI

Serves 6-8

Ingredients
1 cup fine bulgur
1 3/4 liter hot water
1 cup flour
1 egg
1 tbsp red pepper paste
1 tsp ground cumin
1 tsp black pepper
1 tsp salt
1 tbsp olive oil
juice of one lemon

For the sauce
1 cup olive oil
1 tbsp tomato paste
5-6 grated tomatoes
7-8 cloves of garlic (crushed)

For the köfte
Step 1: Place the bulgur with the hot water in a bowl and let it rest until cool. Add the flour, egg, red pepper paste, spices, and salt. Mix well, kneading with your hands until all the ingredients are well incorporated.

Step 2: Moisten your hands with a bit of olive oil, form small balls the size of a cherry, and make a hole in the center by pressing with your fingers. When you have assembled the balls, transfer them to a deep pot that you will have put over medium heat with 1 1/2 liters of water.

Add the lemon juice, check the salt, and cook for about 8 minutes.

For the sauce
Step 3: In a frying pan, heat the olive oil and sauté the tomato paste in the hot oil for 2-3 minutes. Add the crushed tomatoes and garlic. Mix well and cook for two additional minutes.

Finishing your dish
Step 4: Drain your köfte and add them to the tomato sauce. Mix and let them cook for a minute to let them absorb the sauce. Serve hot and decorate with some parsley leaves.

SARI BURMA

(Yellow Twist)

Serves 20

Ingredients
For the syrup
300g sugar
250ml water
1 tbsp lemon juice

For the stuffing
300g ground walnuts
½ cup sugar

For assembling the dish
500g or 20 sheets of filo pastry
1 1/4 cups melted butter

You also will need
1 oklava (thin rolling pin)

Step 1: Preheat the oven to 180°C.
For the syrup

Step 2: Place the sugar and water in a heavy-bottomed saucepan and mix well. Bring to a medium heat and cook for 10 minutes or until it begins to thicken. Add a tablespoon of lemon juice, mix, and remove from heat. Set aside.

For the stuffing
Step 3: Mix the sugar with the ground walnuts. Set aside.

Assembling your dessert:
Step 4: With a brush, coat a sheet of filo pastry with melted butter. Sprinkle some of the walnut stuffing filling over it.

Step 5: Roll out the dough with the walnuts using the oklava. Once it is rolled out, push inwards from both sides towards the center to shrink the roll. Repeat the process with the rest of the filo pastry.

Step 6: Grease a square ovenproof dish with butter and place the rolls in it. Cut into three rows lengthwise and sprinkle them with 1/4 cup melted butter. Bake in the preheated oven for 25–30 minutes or until golden brown. Take out of the oven and pour the syrup over the rolls. Let it rest for 20 minutes before serving to give it a chance to absorb the syrup.

KADAYIF DESSERT

Serves 6-8

Ingredients
For the syrup
300g sugar
250g water
1 tbsp lemon juice

For the kadayıf
250g wire kadayıf
100g butter, plus a little extra to grease the dish
1/4 cup whole pistachios
1/2 + 1/4 cups crushed pistachios

Step 1: Preheat the oven to 200°C.

For the syrup
Step 2: Mix the sugar with the water and cook over medium heat for 10 minutes in a heavy-bottomed pot. Add the lemon juice, mix well, and remove from the heat. Set aside.

For the Kadayıf
Step 3: If the kadayıf is not fresh, spread it out on a tray and drizzle with a bit of water to soften it. Cut the kadayıf threads into 1 cm long pieces.

Step 4: Melt the butter over a low heat and use a little to grease the pan.

Step 5: Place the whole pistachios in the center of the tray and cover them with half of the kadayıf that you previously cut into small pieces. Press down and cover with the powdered pistachios, distributing them over the entire base. Use the rest of the kadayıf to cover the pistachios and press down.

Step 6: Pour in the butter, making sure to cover all the pie, and bake for about 10 minutes or until golden brown. Flip the dessert upside down for double-sided pie cooking and cook for an additional 10 minutes. Remove from the oven and let it rest for two minutes. Cover with the syrup. Garnish with crushed pistachios.

KÜNEFE

Serves 6-8

Ingredients
For the syrup
300g granulated sugar
250ml water
juice of half a lemon

For the künefe
250g kadayıf
100mlg kaymak (thick cream)
1 tbsp butter
1 tsp grape molasses
200gr Dil peyniri (stringy cheese)
1 tsp butter
2 handfuls finely chopped pistachios
1 tsp molasses

For garnishing
Kaymak (thick cream) or Vanilla ice cream

For the syrup
Step 1: In a heavy-bottomed pot, mix the sugar with the water and cook over medium heat for 15-20 minutes or until it begins to thicken. Add the lemon juice, mix well, and remove from the heat. Set aside.

For the künefe
Step 2: Spread the kadayıf on a tray and mix with the kaymak to soften it. Squeeze the kadayıf threads with your hands to cut them into 1 cm thick pieces.

Step 3: Melt the butter, mix with the molasses, and spread this mixture on the bottom of a second pan.

Step 4: Put half of the kadayıf into the pan and press it to compact. Place the cheese evenly over the pie. Make sure to leave a gap around the edges so that the cheese does not spill out when it melts. Cover the cheese thoroughly with the remaining kadayıf and press again to compact the pie. Cook over a medium heat, constantly checking to avoid burning.

Step 5: Once the bottom of your pie is golden brown, use a lid or another pan to flip the dessert upside down so as to cook the other side until golden brown.

Step 6: Remove from heat and let it rest for 2-3 minutes. Spread the syrup over the künefe and sprinkle 2 handfuls of finely chopped pistachios on top. Serve it hot with kaymak or vanilla ice cream.

SOUPS FROM AROUND THE COUNTRY

EZOGELIN ÇORBASI

(Ezogelin soup)

Serves 6

Ingredients
1 medium onion
1 clove garlic
2 tbsp vegetable oil
1 tbsp pepper paste
1 cup red lentils
2 liters hot water
1/2 cup rice
1/2 fresh bulgur
1 tbsp butter
1 tbsp dried mint
1 tsp powdered red chili
Lemon wedges and bread to serve

Step 1: Finely chop the onions and garlic and sauté them with the vegetable oil in a heavy-bottomed pot until the onion turns translucent. Add the red pepper paste, stir and sauté for two additional minutes.

Step 2: Add the lentils, cook for a minute, and add two liters of hot water. Let the lentils cook for five minutes and add the rice and bulgur. Cook until all the grains are al dente.

Step 3: In a small skillet, melt the butter and pour over the dried mint and powdered red pepper powder. Mix well and spread over the soup. Serve hot with some lemon wedges and accompanied with a slice of bread.

YAYLA ÇORBASI

(Spring soup)

Serves 6

Ingredients
For the syrup

1/2 cup rice
8 cups water
1 cup yogurt
1 egg
1 tbsp flour
Salt to taste
2 tbsp butter
1 tbsp dried mint

Step 1: Cook the rice with the water in a heavy-bottomed pot for about 10 minutes or until the rice is al dente.

Step 2: In a bowl, mix the yogurt, egg and flour. Beat and gradually add a cup of the boiling water from the rice pot, constantly mixing to prevent the yogurt from separating.

Step 3: Remove the pot with the rice from the heat and add the yogurt mixture, stirring constantly. Return the pot to the heat, add salt to taste and cook until the ingredients are combined (approximately 5 minutes).

Step 4: In a separate pan, melt the butter and add the dried mint. Cook until it begins to foam. Pour it over the soup and serve hot.

MERCIMEK ÇORBASI
(Red lentil soup)

Serves 6-8

Ingredients
2 cups red lentils
1 big onion – chopped
2 tbsp oil
2 tbsp flour
1 tsp red pepper paste
2 liters vegetable stock
Salt to taste
1 tsp cumin
1 tsp black pepper

For the sauce
2 tbsp butter
1 tsp red pepper powder

For garnishing
Lemon wedges and bread

Step 1: Wash your red lentils well under running cold water. Set aside.

Step 2: In a saucepan, sauté the onions in the oil until they turn translucent. Add the flour and sauté until lightly browned. Add the pepper paste and lentils. Mix well and cook for a few seconds. Add the vegetable stock, mix, and cook over a medium heat until it starts to boil. Lower the heat to a minimum and gently simmer for about 15 minutes.

Step 3: Once the lentils are soft, blend them using a hand blender. Pass them through a strainer if you prefer a smoother soup.

Add salt, cumin, and pepper. Cook for 5 more minutes. Remove from heat.

Preparing the sauce
Step 4: In the meantime, melt the butter in a small pan and add the powdered red chili. Cook until it begins to foam. Pour it over the soup. Serve hot with some lemon wedges and some slices of bread.

ALICIA SANTANA

Alicia Santana is a Dominican chef who specializes in International and Modernist cuisine.

As a food traveler, she visited Nicaragua, Costa Rica, Panama, Guatemala, Mexico, Colombia, Peru, Cuba, İtaly, Belgium, Spain, France, Greece, the Balkans (Albania, Croatia, Montenegro), and Lebanon to learn their gastronomic secrets.

Alicia lived in Turkey during five years and traveled the length and breadth of the country in her eagerness to learn about its gastronomic culture. She graduated as a professional chef from the Turkish Culinary Academy, Alicia volunteered in this institution teaching Latin American Cuisine. Before focusing professionally on the gastronomy world, she graduated with a degree in Social Work and Development Management at the Central American University in Nicaragua – UCA, focused on field research and a thesis on street children's rights and protection.

She also holds diplomas in Food Photography, Food Writing for Publications and Writing and Publishing recipes from Le Cordon Bleu. She was the co-owner and executive chef at La Mesa del Chef Restaurant in Ankara. She has participated in the gastronomic TV program Taste & Spices, broadcasted from Turkey to the entire African continent on Natura TV, and in several gastronomic events in Turkey.

Bibliography

Alvarez, M. (2018, November 15). Pais Dominicano Temático. Retrieved from https://paisdominicanotematico.com/2018/11/15/la-migracion-arabe-a-republica-dominicana/

Ceylan, J. A., & Ozcelik, A. O. (2018). Cuisine culture of the pearl of Mesopotamia: Mardin, Turkey. Ankara: Journal of Ethnic Foods, Ankara University, faculty of Health Sciences.

Foundation, T. C. (n.d.). Turkish-Cuisine. Retrieved from http://www.turkish-cuisine.org/historical-development-1/cuisine-of-central-asian-turks-121/the-homeland-of-the-turks-173.htlm

Hösükoğlu, F. (2021, March 24). History of Gaziantep Gastronomy. (A. Santana, Interviewer)

James A. Duke, M. J.-G.-A. (2003). CRC Handbook of Medicinal Spices. USA: CRC Press.

Nature, I. U. (n.d.). IUCN, International Union for Conservation of Nature. Retrieved from https://www.iucn.org/regions/europe/resources/country-focus/turkey

Oberling, Gerry and Smith, Grace Martin, Food Culture of the Ottoman Palace, Turkish Ministry of Culture, 2001

Rosengarten, F. (1969). The Book of Spices. New York: Jove Publ., İnc.

Sansal, B. (n.d.). All About Turkey. Retrieved from https://www.allaboutturkey.com/index.html

Sürücüoğlü, P. D. (n.d.). Üzüm pekmez (Grape Molasses).

Tezcan, D. M. (n.d.). Turkish Cultural Foundation. Retrieved from Eating Habits of the Turks and Their Associated Behaviors: http://www.turkish-cuisine.org/culinary-culture-202/eating-habits-of-the-turks-199.html?PagingIndex=0

UNESCO. (n.d.). UNESCO. Retrieved from Silk Route Program – What is the spice route? https://es.unesco.org/silkroad/node/8269

GLOSSARY

Aşure

(Noah's pudding) Common in Turkey and other countries of the Middle East and Balkans, it can correctly be described as a 'legendary' pudding. The word aşure comes from the Arabic ashura which means the tenth day of the holy month of Muharram, the first month of the Muslim calendar. It is a wheat pudding made with dried nuts and fruits.

Ayran

This is a Turkish cold beverage made with yogurt, water, and salt, usually served with lamb dishes. It's popular in many Central Asian, Middle Eastern and South-eastern European countries.

Börek

In Turkish and the Middle East – A pie of filo pastry filled with cheese, spinach, or minced meat.

Dolma

Greek, Turkish. Stuffed vegetables, especially eggplant, zucchini and bell pepper stuffed with rice and minced meat.

Dolma Oyacağı

A turkish cooking tool used to core vegetables prior to filling them.

Dolma Tası

This is a perforated clay lid. It's used to cover and compress the dolmas during the cooking process.

Helva

A Helva is an eastern Mediterranean sweet made from crushed sesame seeds and honey. The word comes probably via Yiddish halva or Turkish helva, from Arabic halwa, which means literally 'sweetmeat'.

Kadayıf

This is a tiny pasta, a bit like vermicelli, prepared with flour and water and fed through a machine with a strainer on a very hot rolling tray. In Turkey, kadayıf is the main ingredient of desserts such as Künefe and the dessert that also bears its name, Kadayıf.

Kebab

A dish consisting of of chunks of meat, fish, or vegetables roasted or grilled on a skewer or spit.

Köfte

(In Middle Eastern and Indian cooking) a savoury ball made with minced meat, paneer, or vegetables.

Künefe
See Kadayf.

Lahmacun

A flatbread covered with meat and baked in the oven, which is served throughout Turkey.

Mercimek

A high-protein legume which is dried and then soaked and cooked prior to eating.

Nar ekşisi

Sour pomegranate syrup.

Oklava

This is a small rolling pin widely used in Turkish cuisine. Of much smaller dimensions than the one commonly known in the West, the oklava is the main instrument to prepare most of the Turkish dishes that include dough in its ingredients, including their famous baklava and hundreds of other recipes.

Pekmez

A thick jelly obtained by evaporating grape juice, which is the basis of Turkish delight and other sweet confections.

Peynir

Cheese.

Pilaf

A method of cooking rice that consists of frying it in oil until golden brown and then cooking it in water until it is tender and loose.

Salça

Tomato or red pepper paste.

Simit

A salty bread that resembles brown donuts sprinkled with sesame seeds. It is sold in bakeries, supermarkets, and hot from small roadside stalls across the country.

Sucuk

Dry fermented sausages.

Sumak

It's the fruit of a shrub that bears its name. In Turkey, it is generally harvested in August and September, and then dried before being consumed as a spice.

Tandoor

A large clay oven that is buried in the ground. It is generally used for slow cooking at low temperatures. It is also used in the baking of unleavened bread.

Tarhana

This is a dried fermented soup prepared during the summer when the vegetables are in season. Tomato, pepper, onion, and herbs are cooked until softened and then allowed to dry under the sun. This powdered soup lasts for months and is conserved to be prepared later, during the cold winters.

Yufka

(Filo pastry) is made with flour and is the main ingredient in such famous dishes as baklava and böreks, amongst numerous other recipes.

Zırh

A large knife used to cut meat, mainly for kebabs.

INDEX